# Athletics Challenges

★ sprinting ★ sustained running ★ hurdling ★ relay ★ shot put ★ discus ★ javelin ★
hammer ★ long jump ★ triple jump ★ high jump ★

**How do you motivate even the most reluctant athlete?
How can you improve the technique of all your students?**

*Athletics Challenges* is a practical resource file designed to ensure that *all* students have a positive learning experience in track and field athletics. It provides a wide range of activities and teaching approaches to enable teachers and coaches to promote a climate of inclusion, enjoyment and challenge for young people up to and beyond the age of 16.

Including straightforward guidance on how to use the resources effectively, *Athletics Challenges* is a compendium of ready-to-use, photocopiable activity sheets to use with your students in a wide range of athletics events.

- An introduction to the theory and research that underpins the activities presented in the file.
- Specific warm-up activities and a range of dynamic mobility exercises for the different athletic activities in the file.

> ***Athletics challenges*** activity sheets provide a wide range of running, jumping and throwing activities designed to develop physical literacy, fundamental athletic techniques and personal and social skills.
>
> ***Peer teaching*** activities for a range of athletics events aim to help improve technical understanding and to enhance social and communication skills through peer teaching.
>
> ***Technical guidance*** resource sheets ensure students develop a good understanding of the principles and techniques of running, jumping and throwing through a series of progressive activities and related questions.

*Athletics Challenges* is a complete kit offering an invaluable source of support and ideas for all student and practising physical education teachers, heads of departments, and training and practising professional sports coaches who want to help learners achieve their full potential and lay the foundation for a healthy and physically active lifestyle.

**Dr Kevin Morgan** is Senior Lecturer at the School of Sport, University of Wales Institute, Cardiff (UWIC), UK, where he is also Programme Director of the MSc in Coaching Science.

★ sprinting ★ sustained running ★ hurdling ★ relay ★ shot put ★ discus ★ javelin ★
hammer ★ long jump ★ triple jump ★ high jump ★

'Without hesitation I can state that this is the best received resource material in our programme and our physical education students enthuse about their capacity to take the ideas from the resource and transfer them into successful and effective physical education lessons during their school based practicum.'
*John Sproule, Head of the Institute of Sport, Physical Education & Health Sciences, University of Edinburgh, UK*

# Athletics Challenges

A resource pack for teaching athletics

Second edition

Kevin Morgan

LONDON AND NEW YORK

First edition published 2002
by UWIC Press

This second edition published 2011
by Routledge
2 Park Square, Milton Park, Abingdon, Oxon OX14 4RN

Simultaneously published in the USA and Canada
by Routledge
711 Third Avenue, New York, NY 10017

*Routledge is an imprint of the Taylor & Francis Group, an informa business*

© 2011 Kevin Morgan

The right of Kevin Morgan to be identified as author of this work has been asserted by him in accordance with sections 77 and 78 of the Copyright, Designs and Patents Act 1988.

All rights reserved. The purchase of this copyright material confers the right on the purchasing institution to photocopy pages which bear the photocopy icon and copyright line at the bottom of the page. No other parts of this book may be reprinted or reproduced or utilised in any form or by any electronic, mechanical, or other means, no known or hereafter invented, including photocopying and recording, or in any information storage or retrieval system, without permission in writing from the publishers.

*Trademark notice:* Product or corporate names may be trademarks or registered trademarks, and are used only for identification and explanation without intent to infringe.

*British Library Cataloguing in Publication Data*
A catalogue record for this book is available from the British Library

*Library of Congress Cataloging-in-Publication Data*
Morgan, Kevin, 1964–
Athletics challenges : a resource pack for teaching athletics / Kevin Morgan. — 2nd ed.
　p. cm.
Includes bibliographical references.
1. Track and field—Study and teaching. 2. Track and field—Training. 3. Track and field—Coaching. 4. Physical education and training—Study and teaching. I. Title.
GV1060.5.M625 2011
796.4207—dc22
2010041745

ISBN13: 978-0-415-58442-5 (pbk)

Typeset in Gill Sans

by FiSH Books, Enfield

# Contents

| | |
|---|---|
| **Foreword** | ix |
| **Introduction** | 1 |
| **Section 1: Warm-ups** | 9 |
| **Section 2: Athletics challenges sheets** | 15 |

*Student resource sheets for a variety of running, jumping and throwing activities designed to develop physical literacy, fundamental athletics techniques and personal and social skills*

| | |
|---|---|
| Sprinting | 21 |
| Sustained running | 33 |
| Hurdling | 45 |
| Relays | 57 |
| Long jump | 69 |
| Triple jump | 81 |
| High jump | 93 |
| Shot put | 105 |
| Discus | 117 |
| Javelin | 129 |
| Hammer | 141 |

| | |
|---|---|
| **Section 3: Peer teaching sheets** | 153 |

*Student resource sheets designed to improve technical understanding in a range of athletics events and to enhance social and communication skills through peer teaching*

| | |
|---|---|
| Sprint starts | 155 |
| Sprinting | 156 |
| Sustained running | 157 |
| Hurdling | 158 |
| Relays: Upsweep exchange | 159 |
| Relays: Downsweep exchange | 160 |
| Long jump: Stride jump | 161 |
| Triple jump | 162 |
| High jump: Fosbury flop | 163 |
| Shot put: Standing put | 164 |
| Discus: Standing throw | 165 |
| Javelin: Standing throw | 166 |

## CONTENTS

**Section 4: Technical guidance sheets** — 167

*Student resource sheets for a variety of running, jumping and throwing activities designed to develop physical literacy, fundamental athletics techniques and personal and social skills*

| | |
|---|---|
| Sprint starts | 170 |
| Sprinting | 171 |
| Sprint hurdling | 172 |
| Sprint relays | 173 |
| Long jump | 174 |
| Triple jump | 175 |
| High jump | 176 |
| Shot put | 177 |
| Discus | 178 |
| Javelin | 179 |

*References* — 181

In loving memory of Dad who always believed in me
and to Mam for her continuous love and support.
Together, they created fantastic motivational climate
and gave me a wonderful start in life.

Illustrations reprinted, with permission, from G. Carr, 1999, *Fundamentals of track and field*, 2nd ed. (Champaign, IL: Human Kinetics).

# Foreword

*Athletics Challenges* is a joy to read for coaches, teachers, and researchers alike. With this resource pack, Dr Kevin Morgan has elegantly taken complex theoretical constructs and artfully used them to inform readers of effective ways to teach and coach athletics. Rarely do research articles in professional journals or practitioner focused instructional texts explicitly inform readers of the relationship between research and practice as succinctly or clearly as *Athletics Challenges*. Indeed, Dr Morgan has certainly made a significant and positive contribution to both the physical education and coaching world with this resource pack.

Readers will quickly notice that the organization and writing of this resource pack is a departure from many similar texts. The reader is introduced to a research based perspective on developing instructional tools that were written to be immediately used by practitioners who desire to be effective in teaching various track and field skills. Woven throughout the text are concepts related to movement literacy in the context of developing deep learning and understanding as well as the technical skills associated with athletics.

From the beginning of the text, the introductory section of *Athletics Challenges* includes a tutorial on the constructs of Achievement Goal Theory and how these constructs relate to developing motivational climates in the physical education and sport setting which promote both success and learning among students and athletes. Drawing from his own and other research, Dr Morgan clearly describes a research based method of developing a mastery oriented motivational climate using the TARGET (Task, Authority, Grouping, Evaluation, and Time) approach widely accepted by researchers as the optimal learning environment within the physical education or sport setting. This research based perspective is a defining element of this resource packet that differentiates it from other texts which only include drills that may or may not be meaningful to students beyond a mere skill based exercise or drill. The addition of a 'life skills' focus further enhances the learning potential of this section and moves it further beyond the development of athletic techniques.

Following the introduction, the four sections found in the packet include a warm-up section, a section on the various athletics challenges, a section describing peer teaching practices, and a final section that includes technical guidance sheets to facilitate deep learning through the discovery process. In the warm-up section, readers learn to engage students in dynamic and continuous movement warm-ups which represent the most current knowledge on effective warm-up routines. The second section is packed with clearly written activities that can be immediately used within the learning setting. The activities were further designed to explicitly foster a mastery-oriented motivational climate to maximize the learning potential of the activity and enhance student learning. It is in the third section where readers learn to use peer teaching in an effective manner to facilitate effective student learning. Finally, the fourth section provides teachers and coaches with technical guidance sheets that facilitate deep student learning through a guided discovery experience.

# FOREWORD ■ ■ ■ ■

Teachers and coaches using the information found within *Athletics Challenges* will find the material valuable in developing effective lessons and sport practices that will improve student learning. Because the information draws upon a well-established research base, the outcomes of the learning experiences are likely to produce even greater student learning than drills found in similar texts. In addition, teachers who find themselves working within the constraints of such things as national curricula or mandates to demonstrate student success will be able to use the information in this resource packet to accomplish those objectives. As a result, *Athletics Challenges*, is both a valuable tool for the teacher or coach and it is a noteworthy example of bridging research and practice to improve teacher effectiveness.

Dr John R. Todorovich
University of West Florida
USA

# Introduction

The materials presented in this teaching resource pack are a product of the author's doctoral research into motivational climate in physical education (PE) (Morgan, 2000; Morgan, 2003; Morgan and Carpenter, 2002; Morgan et al., 2005) and over 20 years of practical athletics teaching experience in schools and universities. The primary aim is to ensure that all students have a positive learning experience in track and field athletics lessons and equal opportunity to learn and achieve their full potential. In order to achieve this, the motivational climate in athletics lessons needs to foster inclusion, enjoyment and individual challenge. The purpose of this resource pack is to provide a range of athletic activities and teaching approaches that will enable PE teachers to promote such a learning climate.

Movement literacy is also a key learning focus and, as such, the activities are specifically designed to develop fundamental running, jumping and throwing skills that form the basis of all sports and lay the foundation for a healthy and physically active lifestyle. The development of students' life skills is a further intended learning outcome, with a specific focus on the personal and social skills of communication, interpersonal skills, decision-making, critical thinking and self-management behaviours (Mandigo et al., 2008). Finally, a range of teaching methods and strategies is promoted to develop 'whole learning', which incorporates the physical, cognitive, social and affective learning domains (Kay, 2003).

The intended learning outcomes are to:

- assist PE teachers in fostering a 'mastery' motivational climate in athletics lessons, focused on self-referenced effort and improvement, in order to promote inclusion and enable all students to achieve success;
- promote movement literacy as the foundation for all sports, and a healthy and active lifestyle;
- develop the life skills of communication, interpersonal skills, decision-making, critical thinking and self-management behaviours;
- foster 'whole learning' in the physical, affective, social and cognitive domains through the use of different teaching methods.

This introduction will focus initially and primarily on motivational climate theory and teaching strategies, but will also touch upon the areas of life skills and whole learning, and give some guidance on how to use the resource pack.

## Promoting a mastery motivational climate

Creating a motivational climate that encourages all students, regardless of their athletic ability, to exert maximum effort in athletics lessons is a difficult challenge for PE teachers and coaches. This is particularly the case when students are over 11 years old and are able to differentiate between effort and ability (Nicholls, 1978). According to Nicholls, up until the age of about 11, children conceive of ability in a self-referenced manner as learning through effort. Later, however, they recognise that the outcome depends on both ability and effort, so that when athletics lessons encourage a public display of ability and evaluate students in relation to normative standards, exerting effort that does not result in a successful performance compared to others in the class is often perceived as failure. In order to avoid this situation many students withdraw effort or attempt to devalue the task, particularly when their perceived ability is low (Ames, 1984). One way to avoid this comparative and potentially demotivating situation is to foster a teaching climate that emphasises self-referenced improvement and effort, so that all students can achieve success.

According to Ames (1984), the motivational climate that teachers create influences the thoughts and feelings of the students and the meaning of success and failure. Two climates have been found to be predominant in educational environments: a competitive or ego climate and an individualistic or mastery climate. In an ego climate comparison with others is the primary source of information for self-evaluation. The focus is on winning or losing and improvement is of little or no significance. In lessons, competition is evident through normatively based assessment, grouping by ability, publicly charting pupils' progress and rewarding those individuals who exhibit high ability. A normative assessment of ability is, therefore, prevalent, so that, if an individual tries hard but doesn't succeed in comparison to others in the class, low ability is implied (ibid.). This type of ego-oriented motivational climate is frequently evident in 'traditional' athletics lessons, which use normative standards as the basis for student assessment. Research in athletics lessons in schools (Carpenter and Morgan, 1999) has revealed that students' perceptions of an ego climate are related to less enjoyment, greater boredom, the belief that success is due to ability rather than effort and a more negative attitude toward athletic activities.

By contrast, in a mastery motivational climate each individual's attainment of rewards is independent of the attainment of rewards by others and performance is evaluated in terms of personal mastery (Ames, 1984). The focus is on comparing new performances with past performances and on improvement through effort. Learning and mastery of the task are the targets, so that prior performances become salient in setting goals and expectations. The structure is characterised by instructing individuals to try their best and to set goals that exceed their own past performances. Comparison is with the self and not normative, as in the ego climate. Perceptions of a mastery climate in school athletics lessons have been found to be related to high satisfaction and low boredom, high perceived ability and intrinsic motivation, the belief that success is due to effort and a more positive attitude toward the activities (Carpenter and Morgan, 1999). These findings suggest that understanding and promoting a particular motivational climate is central to student learning and motivation in athletics lessons. Furthermore, research has found that a mastery motivational climate is likely to result in improved physical activity levels in young people (Parish et al., 2007).

The teaching structures that underlie a mastery climate were identified by Ames (1992), based on the six areas of task, authority, rewards, grouping, evaluation and timing (TARGET) that were originally introduced by Epstein (1989) (see Table 1). Manipulating the TARGET structures to be more mastery focused has been found to improve students' motivation in athletics lessons (Morgan and Carpenter, 2002), resulting in greater satisfaction with the activities, a more positive attitude towards athletics and a preference for more challenging tasks. Thus, one way to enhance motivation in athletics lessons is to implement the TARGET teaching structures in such a way as to promote a mastery climate. The TARGET structures are, therefore, suggested as the primary underpinning principles in this resource pack. The following research-based practical suggestions are suggested to help foster a mastery motivational climate in athletics lessons. It is acknowledged, however, given the constraints and often 'messy' reality of PE teaching and coaching, that it will not always be possible to adhere to these TARGET guidelines and, as such, they should be viewed as underpinning structures and principles to work towards rather than essential components of every lesson.

**Table 1** TARGET structures in athletics lessons

| TARGET DESCRIPTION | TEACHING SUGGESTIONS |
|---|---|
| Task | • Students set self- or group-referenced goals for improvement<br>• Design tasks for variety, differentiation and inclusion |
| Authority | • Students involved in decision-making and task design |
| Recognition | • Private individual recognition and feedback on improvement and effort |
| Grouping | • Mixed-ability, co-operative groups |
| Evaluation | • Self-referenced – based on performance, improvement and effort scores<br>• Students keep personal diaries to record performances |
| Timing | • Flexible time to complete tasks<br>• Promotion of maximum participation within lessons |

## Applying the TARGET structures

### Task

Encourage students to set self-referenced or group-referenced goals for improvement in the various athletic activities. This will emphasise the mastery focus of the lessons and define success as improvement on previous best performances, thus allowing all students to achieve success. That is not to say that competition between students should be eliminated, as this can be a very effective means of motivation for those who are competitively oriented and have high perceived ability, but that competition against others should not be emphasised by the teacher. Instead teachers should encourage all students to strive to improve their personal best achievements and those who want to compete against others should have the opportunity to do so, if the respective individuals are happy to engage. Choice is a key element here, but the underlying message from the teacher to the students should be about personal improvement and not finding out who the best performers are in the class.

The public display of ability, which is evident when the whole class take it in turns to perform the same activity, can be very threatening to students who do not compare favourably with others in the class and have a low perception of their own ability. Think here of the traditional high jump lesson where students attempt the jumps one at a time in front of the whole class and are eliminated on their failures at different heights. In such circumstances, lower-ability students and those who have a competitive orientation are likely to withdraw effort or devalue the task to avoid embarrassment in front of their peers (Ames, 1984).

Reducing the public display of ability by providing a number of activities within each lesson may, therefore, help to improve the students' motivation and effort within lessons and promote a more positive attitude towards the activity. A multi-dimensional lesson design, so that either a number of different athletic events are taking place simultaneously, as in a multi-event (see Figure 1) or multi-station (see Figure 2) lesson design, can help to de-emphasise the comparative element. Alternatively, the same task can be practised by a number of small sub-groups simultaneously in different areas of the working space. This type of lesson design also reduces time waiting for turns and encourages maximum activity in lessons. It is also imperative that tasks should be differentiated, so that they are achievable by all students at their own level. Furthermore, allowing an element of choice in the activities promotes inclusion and decision-making skills.

## *Authority*

Involve students in decision-making within lessons as this is another important aspect in creating a mastery climate and one that helps to promote the life skills of communication and interpersonal skills. This focus on allowing students to make choices within lessons also promotes the planning and decision-making aspects of PE, which are often neglected in athletics lessons. Thus, for example, based on 'pacing' progressions, students could work out the pace at which they should run each 100m of an 800m time trial or the method of relay baton exchange that best suits their team. Student involvement in their own learning has been shown to be an effective motivational strategy within athletics lessons (Morgan and Carpenter, 2002).

## *Recognition and evaluation*

Recognise and evaluate students on individual improvement and effort within lessons so that everyone has equal opportunity to be successful, regardless of their athletic ability. Consistent with the task structure, all students should strive to improve their personal best achievements. In order to enhance this focus on improvement and effort, personal diaries or score sheets (see Figure 3) can be used for recording performances, as well as self-rated effort and improvement within lessons. This type of approach can help students to develop self-management behaviours and a sense of responsibility, which can help future lifestyle decisions (Fox and Harris, 2003).

## *Grouping*

Ames (1992) recommends the use of mixed ability co-operative groups and frequent changes of groups as this allows students to work with a variety of others to set and meet personal and group targets. This type of grouping structure can also involve the students in a number of roles including performer, coach, official and leader, thus broadening the learning outcomes and developing more holistic learning (Kay, 2003). However, research (Morgan and Carpenter, 2002; Morgan et al., 2005) hasn't always supported mixed-ability groups in athletics and has suggested that, for activities such as sustained running, it is less comparative for students to be in self-chosen ability based groups than mixed-ability groups where the differences in ability are immediately evident for all to see.

■ ■ ■ ■ INTRODUCTION

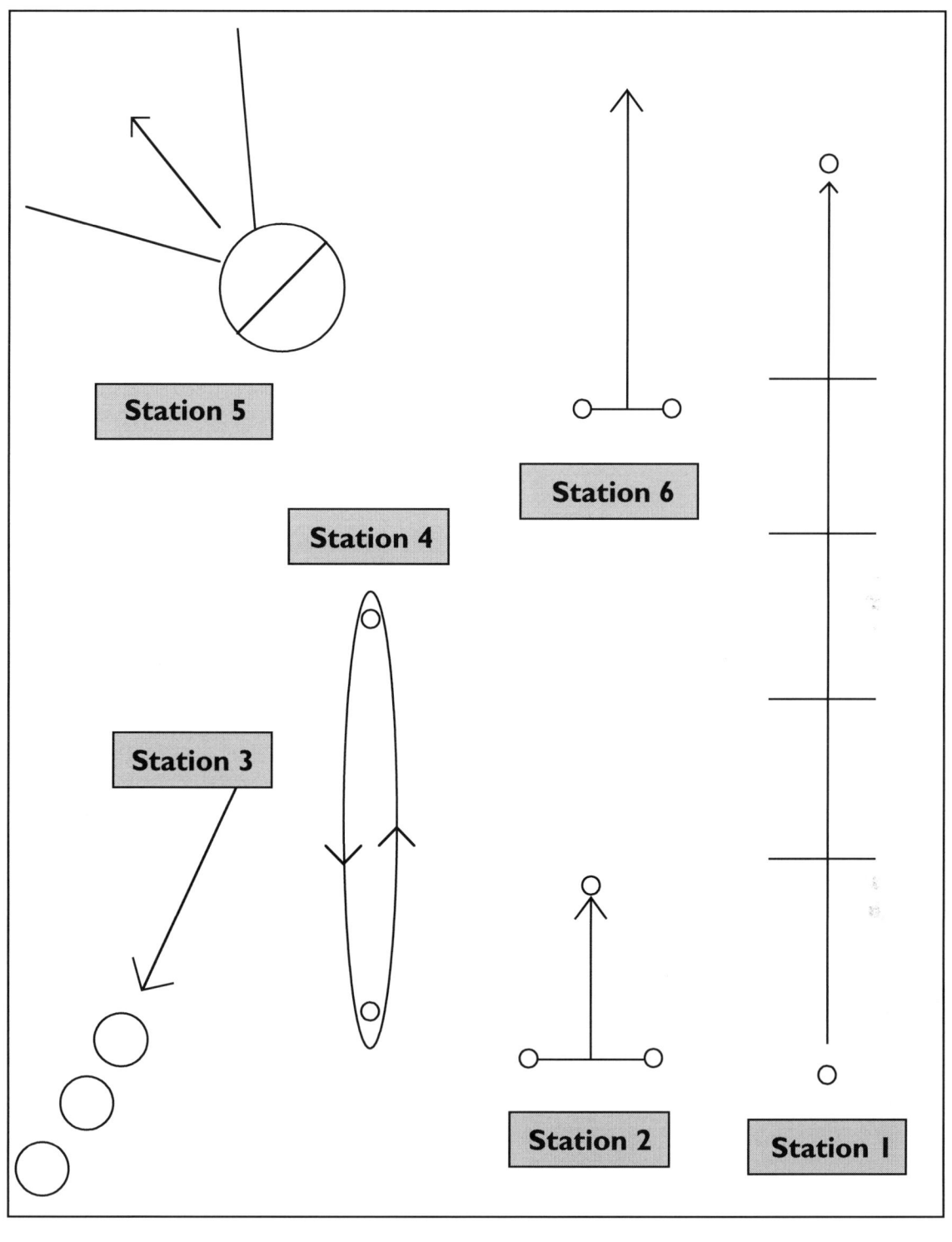

**Station 1** Hurdling challenge 4
**Station 2** Long jump challenge 1
**Station 3** Javelin challenge 3
**Station 4** Sprinting challenge 1
**Station 5** Shot put challenge 2
**Station 6** Triple jump challenge 1

**Figure 1** Multi-event lesson

ATHLETICS CHALLENGES ■ ■ ■ ■

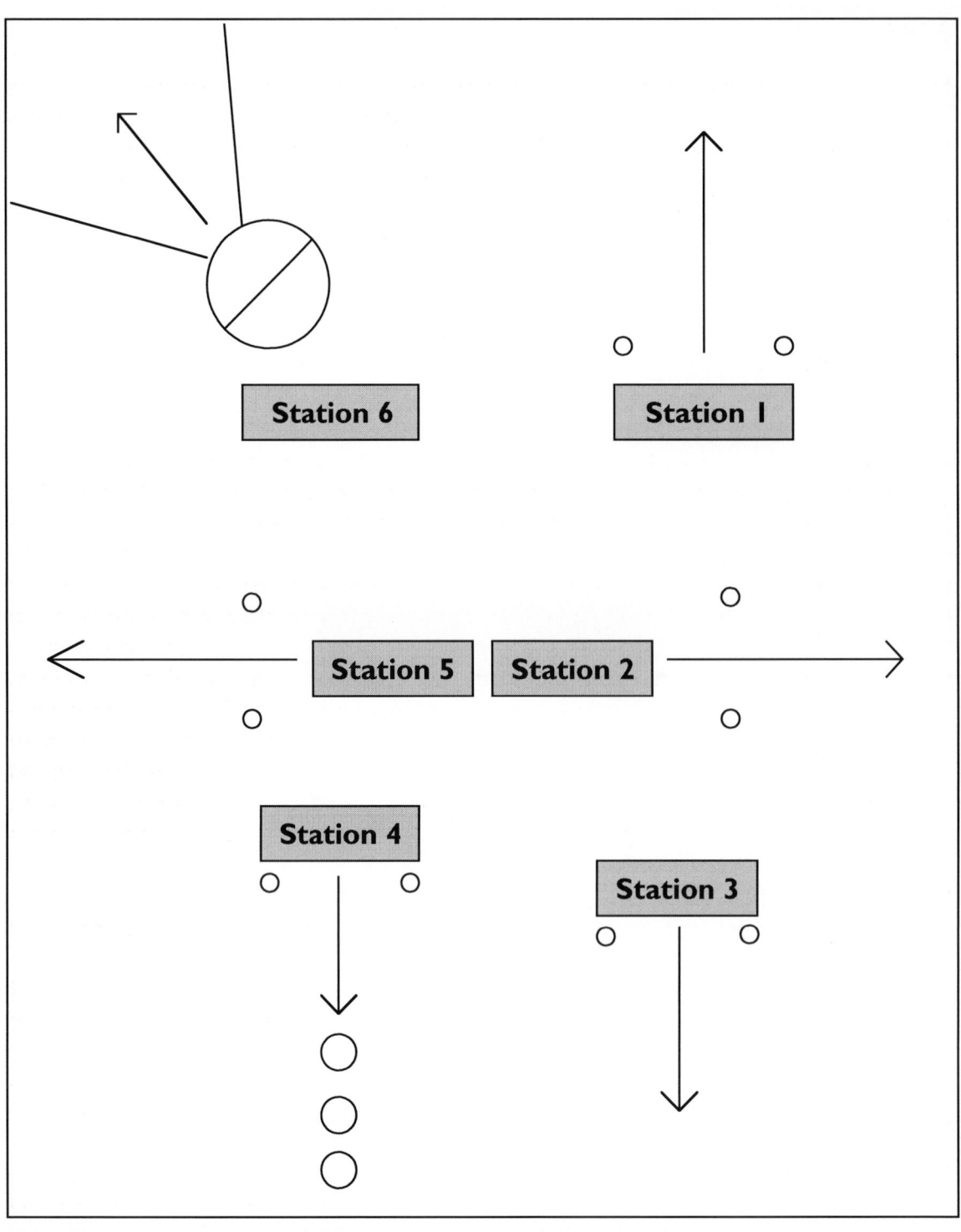

**Station 1** Shot put challenge 1
**Station 2** Shot put challenge 2
**Station 3** Shot put challenge 3
**Station 4** Shot put challenge 4
**Station 5** Shot put challenge 5
**Station 6** Shot put challenge 6

**Figure 2** Multi-station shot put lesson

# INTRODUCTION

## *Time*

Maximising activity time is an important focus of the challenge approach to athletics teaching and this is often best achieved by the multi-dimensional organisation referred to in the Task structure which helps to avoid long periods of waiting for a turn. The other important aspect of the time structure is allowing flexible time to complete tasks, so that students can work at different rates, thus encouraging further differentiation. Allowing flexible time for activities, where students progress at their own preferred pace, does, however, present logistical issues in lessons and may not always be possible, or advisable, depending on the nature of the class and/or the activity.

## Developing life skills

Physical education is viewed as an ideal vehicle for the development of life skills as a mechanism for developing physical activity behaviours in young people (Fox and Harris, 2003; Morgan, 2004; Mandigo *et al.*, 2008). According to Mandigo *et al.*, the life skills of communication, interpersonal skills, decision-making, critical thinking and self-management are crucial in developing healthy and positive young people. Furthermore, Fox and Harris (2003) identified helping students to develop self-management skills that equip them to make lifestyle changes and creating a learning environment in which students can develop a sense of responsibility as key features of a successful health-related exercise programme.

Adhering to the TARGET structures provides numerous opportunities for the development of such life skills. For example, teaching students to set self-referenced goals within tasks and to evaluate their own progress can develop decision-making, critical thinking and self-management skills. These same life skills could be further developed by manipulating the authority and time structures so that students are encouraged to make informed choices and manage their own time more effectively. Communication and interpersonal skills can be enhanced by authority and grouping structures that encourage students to take on leadership roles and interact co-operatively with others. Furthermore, self-management skills can be enhanced by teacher recognition of self-referenced effort and progress.

A key feature of this resource pack is the identification of these key life skills on each of the athletic challenges task cards. The primary purpose of this feature is to educate students about the life skills they are developing in their athletics lessons and to provide a prompt for teachers to highlight these skills to the students and discuss their importance in relation to developing healthy lifestyles and positive behaviours. Additionally, promoting fundamental movement literacy and core skills in running, jumping and throwing as the foundation for all sport and physical activity can act as a strong motivator for many students to engage in athletics lessons and help to develop a level of movement literacy that will enable them to lead a physically active lifestyle (Whitehead, 2010).

## Teaching methods and 'whole learning'

Consistent with a life skills focus and a student-centred approach to teaching, the development of 'whole learning' involves educating the child in, through and about the physical in four central domains, namely the physical, social, cognitive and affective (Kay, 2003). In order to achieve these different learning outcomes, the use of a variety of teaching methods is considered to be an essential element of this resource. Previous research by the author (Morgan *et al.*, 2005) has found that the reciprocal and discovery teaching styles (Mosston and Ashworth, 2002) were strongly associated with mastery teaching behaviours and positive student responses in athletics lessons. Building on this research, peer teaching and technical guidance resource sheets have been designed to emphasise the social, cognitive and affective learning domains, in addition to the physical.

## How to use the resource pack

This resource pack contains four main sections: warm-ups, athletics challenges, peer teaching sheets and technical guidance sheets.

Athletics challenges sheets are student resource sheets for a variety of running, jumping and throwing activities designed to develop physical literacy, fundamental athletics techniques and personal and social skills.

Peer teaching sheets are student resource sheets designed to improve technical understanding in a range of athletics events and enhance social and communication skills through peer teaching.

Technical guidance sheets are student resource sheets designed to develop a good understanding of the principles and techniques of running, jumping and throwing through a series of progressive activities and related questions.

Each section begins with 'teacher notes' providing a set of guidelines on how to use the resources in order to achieve the intended learning outcomes. All the resources in this pack are designed for students aged 10–14, but could also be used as practices and progressions for older or slightly younger students.

# Section 1

# Warm-ups

This section provides examples of specific warm-up activities and a range of dynamic mobility exercises for different track and field events. Firstly, the continuous warm-up phase at the beginning of the lesson is considered. The intention here is to provide alternatives to the traditional 'jog around the track', which is repetitive and can result in an ego-focused class climate where running ability is emphasised rather than effective warm-up principles. Alternative examples of activity-specific continuous warm-up activities are provided in the first part of this section.

Traditionally, static stretching has been used at the beginning of sessions, following the low-intensity continuous activity. However, this interrupts the natural flow of an optimum warm-up and does not prepare the students effectively for the dynamic movements that will follow. The second part of this section, therefore, gives examples of dynamic mobility exercises to follow the continuous low-intensity phase of the warm-up.

## Continuous warm-up activities

The following activities are designed to get all students working continuously for about three to five minutes without thinking about how far they are actually running and without making direct comparisons with other members of the class. Remind the students that a warm-up is not a race. The first set of generic warm-up activities are for any athletic event, and the second set are examples of event-specific warm-ups.

## Generic warm-up activities

- Jogging around the outside of a marked area (approx 30m x 30m square) in single-file formation in a clockwise or anti-clockwise direction, alternating the jog with side-stepping, cross-over steps, jogging backwards, heel flicks, forward skipping, backward skipping, arm swings in circles, or any other variations. Change direction.

- Jogging anywhere in a marked area (approx 30m x 30m square), alternating the jog with side-stepping, cross-over steps, jogging backwards, heel flicks, forward skipping, backward skipping, arm swings in circles, or any other variations.

- Follow a partner anywhere in a marked area (approx 30m x 30m square), alternating the jog with side-stepping, cross-over steps, jogging backwards, heel flicks, forward skipping, backward skipping, arm swings in circles, or any other variations. Change the leader.

## ATHLETICS CHALLENGES ■ ■ ■ ■

- Jogging on a marked zig-zag course (as below) in a single-file formation, alternating the jog with side-stepping, cross-over steps, jogging backwards, heel flicks, forward skipping, backward skipping, arm swings in circles, or any other variations whenever a new cone is passed.

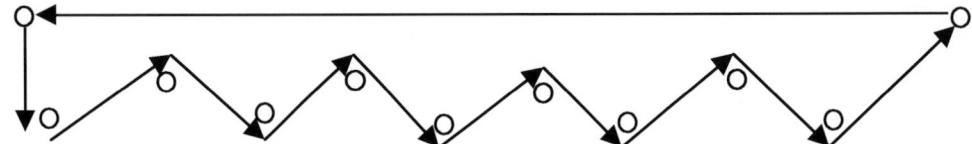

- In small groups (4–6), jogging around a running track in single-file formation, taking it in turns to run to the front and then slowing down to a jogging pace.

- In small groups (4–6), jogging around a running track whilst talking it in turns to choose a topic to talk about for one minute. Change the topic after each minute.

## Event-specific warm-up activities

### Sustained running

- In small groups (4–6), start by standing in single-file formation in a marked area (approx 10/15m x 10/15m). On the teacher's command, jog out of the area in single-file and estimate 15 seconds to run anywhere and return into the area. Increase the time to 30 seconds, 45 seconds and 1 minute.

### Sprints

- Following a continuous warm-up activity and dynamic mobility exercises, jog forwards and, on command, drop to touch the floor with two hands and sprint for three to five strides. Repeat several times on a straight running area.

- Following a continuous warm-up activity and dynamic mobility exercises, jog forwards and, on command, turn 180 degrees with a small jump, drop to touch the floor with two hands and sprint for three to five strides in the opposite direction. Repeat several times.

- Following a continuous warm-up activity and dynamic mobility exercises, jog slowly backwards and, on command, drop to touch the floor with two hands and sprint forwards for three to five strides. Repeat several times.

### Relays

- In groups of four, jogging around a running track in single-file formation whilst continuously transferring a relay baton from the back of the group to the front. When the baton gets to the front of the group the front person drops to the back and starts the baton transfer process again.

- Follow a partner anywhere in a marked area (approx 30m x 30m square). On command, try to get away from your partner.

## WARM-UPS

### Hurdles

- Jogging over lines of dome cones (as shown below), stepping over them with your right and left legs leading to establish a preferred lead leg.

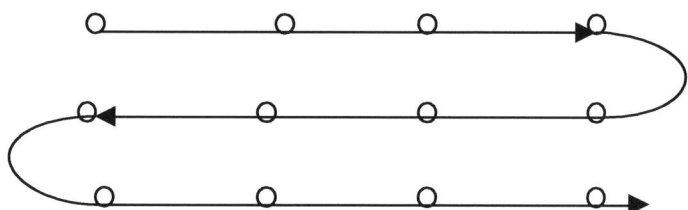

### Long/triple jump

- Jogging anywhere in a marked area (approx 20/30m x 20/30m square) with numerous dome cones randomly placed within the area, stepping and jumping over the cones using different take-offs and landings including 1 foot to 2 feet, 2 to 1, 1 to other, 1 to the same (hopping) and 2 to 2. Jumps should not be too dynamic for this phase. Practise landing safely and controlled, and don't look down at the cones.

### High jump

- Jogging around a marked area (approx 30m x 30m square), jumping off a one-foot take-off to reaching for a target, or try to head an object (e.g. a suspended football) at various points around the area. Change direction and take-off foot to establish preferred take-off.

### Shot

- In groups of three, jogging across a 15/20m area in a shuttle run formation performing drills such as heel flicks, high knees, cross-over and side-stepping whilst holding a weighted ball or large ball above your head, or performing shoulder-to-shoulder pushes, chest pushes or any other variations holding the ball. Hand the ball to the next person in the group.

- In groups of four to six, standing in zig-zag formation passing a weighted ball or large ball along the line using a push pass above head height and then jogging to the end of the line to receive the next pass.

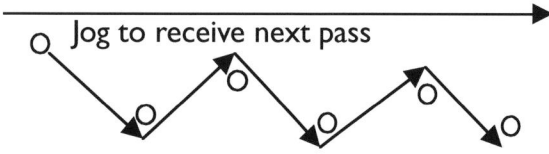

ATHLETICS CHALLENGES ■ ■ ■ ■

## *Discus*

- Jogging on a marked zig-zag course (as below) in a single-file formation, alternating the jog with side-stepping, cross-over steps, forward skipping, arm swings in circles, or any other variations linked to discus throwing whenever a new cone is passed.

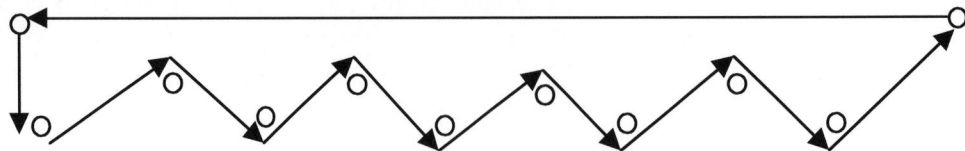

## *Javelin*

- In groups of three, jogging across a 20/30m area in a shuttle run formation whilst holding a small ball performing the following drills:
  - high knees holding the ball resting on the shoulder of your preferred throwing arm, palm upwards, as in a javelin carry position
  - cross-over steps holding the ball with your arm fully withdrawn, palm for up, as in the pre-delivery javelin throw position
  - alternating between high knees with the ball on your shoulder and cross-over steps with your arm fully withdrawn

## *Throwing game*

- Following a continuous warm-up activity and dynamic mobility exercises, two teams of students standing on lines 15/20m apart, with a basketball placed on the ground equi-distant from both lines (as shown below). Both teams throw volleyballs/soccer balls at the basketball, attempting to hit it over their opponents' line using one- or two-handed 'pull' throws from above the head only for javelin, 'push' throws from the chest for shot or 'sling' throws from the side of the body for discus.

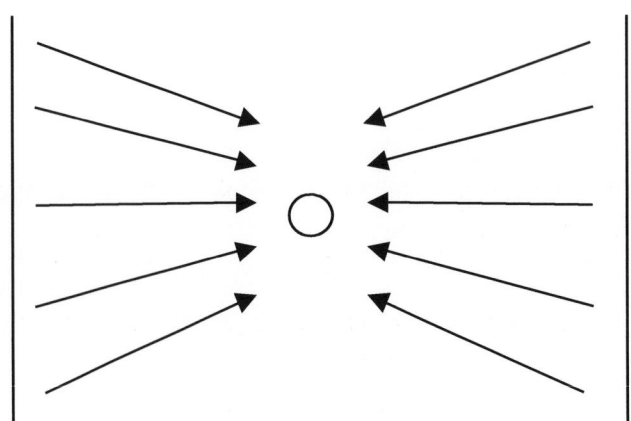

## Dynamic mobility exercises

The following is a range of upper- and lower-body mobility exercises suitable for all athletic activities. Depending on the practical focus of the lesson, students complete all the exercises in a systematic routine working from head to feet, or choose the most specific exercises for the activity to follow. The teacher introduces the exercises at the beginning of the unit and, in accordance with a mastery authority structure (Ames, 1992), students take responsibility for their own exercise routines as the teaching unit progresses. Students perform the movements described below as smoothly as possible and progress from a small to large range of movement and a slow to fast speed.

### Upper body

*Neck mobility:*

- Flexion/extension – Tuck your chin on your chest and then lift the chin upwards as far as possible. Perform 6–10 repetitions.

- Rotation – Turn your chin laterally towards your right shoulder and then towards your left shoulder. Perform 6–10 repetitions.

- Lateral flexion – Lower your right ear towards your right shoulder and then your left ear towards your left shoulder. Perform 6–10 repetitions.

*Arm swings:*

- Overhead – Swing both arms continuously to an overhead position and then forwards, downwards and backwards, or backwards, downwards and forwards. Perform 6–10 repetitions in each direction.

- Front cross-overs – Swing both arms out to your sides and then cross them in front of your chest. Perform 6–10 repetitions.

- Sprint arms – With your hands cupped, resting your thumb against your first finger and your arms bent to 90 degrees at the elbow, swing your arms forwards and backwards to the side of your body repeatedly. Stop the hand at shoulder height in front of your body and drive the elbow backwards until your upper arm is parallel to the ground. Perform 6–10 repetitions for each arm.

*Shoulder girdle and trunk movements:*

- Flexion/extension – Slump (protract) your shoulders by tucking your chin towards your chest, then pull your shoulders back (retract), raising your chin, lifting your chest and slightly arching your back. Perform 6–10 repetitions.

- Lateral flexion – With your arms at your sides, bend sideways at the waist to your right and then to the left. Perform 6–10 repetitions.

- Rotation – With hands in front of your chest and elbows out to the sides, twist at your waist to the right and then back to the left. Perform 6–10 repetitions.

### Lower body

*Hips:*

- Circles – With feet shoulder width apart and hands on your hips, make circles with your hips in a clockwise direction and then repeat in an anti-clockwise direction. Perform 6–10 repetitions in each direction.

*Upper legs:*

- Heel flicks – Standing upright or leaning against a barrier or partner for support, lift your right heel repeatedly towards your seat, whilst supporting your body weight on your left leg. Repeat for the left leg. Perform 6–10 repetitions for each leg.

- Knee lifts – Standing upright or leaning against a barrier or partner for support, lift your right knee repeatedly towards your chest, whilst supporting your body weight on your left leg. Repeat for the left leg. Perform 6–10 repetitions for each leg.

- Leg swings flexion/abduction – Leaning slightly forward with your weight on your left leg and both hands on a support for balance, swing your right leg side-to-side repeatedly. Repeat for the left leg. Perform 6–10 repetitions for each leg.

- Leg swings flexion/extension – With your weight on your left leg and your right hand on a support for balance, swing your right leg forwards and backwards repeatedly. Repeat for the left leg. Perform 6–10 repetitions for each leg.

*Lower legs:*

- Double-leg ankle bounces – Leaning slightly forwards with your hands on a barrier and your weight on your toes, raise and lower both heels repeatedly (bounce). Perform 6–10 repetitions.

- Single-leg ankle bounces – Leaning slightly forwards with your hands on a barrier and your weight on your toes, raise the right heel then left heel alternately and repeatedly. Perform 6–10 repetitions for each leg.

### Cool down

At the end of the lesson, jog continuously or vary this by alternating the jog with side-skipping, cross-over steps, jogging backwards, heel flicks, forward skipping, backward skipping, arm swings in circles, or any other variations. Use a range of static stretches of the main muscle groups that have been used in the lesson. Focus on relaxing and lengthening the muscles to bring the body back to a state of rest.

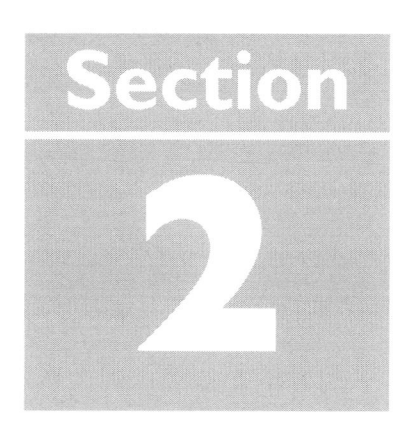

# Section 2: Athletics challenges sheets

## Teacher notes

The athletics challenges resource sheets include a variety of running, jumping and throwing activities designed to develop the fundamental movement skills for specific track and field events. The challenges are organised into sprinting, sustained running, hurdling, relay, long jump, triple jump, high jump, shot, discus, javelin and hammer activities.

The intended learning outcomes of this section are to:

- develop fundamental movement literacy in running, jumping and throwing;
- foster a mastery motivational climate and encourage students to focus upon achieving personal best performances in a range of athletic activities suitable to their age and physical development;
- develop the life skills of communication, interpersonal skills, decision-making, critical thinking and self-management behaviours.

## How to use the cards

The teacher makes the decisions about the lesson objectives; organises the student groupings, equipment and space; hands out the sheets; and demonstrates the challenges or organises the students to do so after they have had time to read the sheets. Students should work in small co-operative groups and take it in turns to perform and assist others in their group by placing cones, and timing, measuring and providing technical feedback tips from the sheets. During the lessons students have the authority to make choices, such as when to start and stop, how many repetitions they complete, the distances they cover or the weight of implements they throw. This is consistent with mastery task, authority and time structures (Ames, 1992 – see the Introduction for a more detailed description of the TARGET structures). The challenge approach allows the teacher to move freely between the groups and to give private feedback, which is consistent with mastery recognition and evaluation structures (ibid.). The overall aim is to foster a student-centred mastery learning environment, where students work co-operatively to maximise their learning opportunities and athletic performances.

As identified in the Introduction, the teacher can select the different athletics challenges so that they all relate to the same event, with the full version of the event being part of the lesson (e.g. use all the shot put challenge sheets) (see Figure 2 in the Introduction). Alternatively, the teacher could organise a multi-event challenge lesson (see Figure 1), where students participate in a number of challenges, each focusing on different athletics events. A further option is for all students in the class to practise the same challenge individually, in pairs, or in small groups (e.g. all doing triple jump challenge 1). The students can choose where to practise (providing the space is safe) and when to start and stop in order to avoid the public display of ability and to encourage maximum participation.

Health and safety implications are identified on the challenge sheets for the students to follow and the teacher to monitor. However, if actual throwing implements, such as shot or javelin, are used (as opposed to safe equipment), the teacher would need to position him/herself to be able to carefully monitor this challenge to ensure that the safety procedures are being adhered to. For some challenges (e.g. high jump 6, shot put 6, discus 6, javelin 6 and hammer 6), there is also a need for students to have been taught the appropriate technical progressions in previous lessons. This is primarily for health and safety reasons but also for sound principles of skill acquisition.

In order to promote inclusion by focusing on self-referenced improvement and effort, a personal athletics diary, or score sheet (Figure 3) can be used with the challenge sheets so that personal best achievements can be recorded and individual targets for improvement set for future attempts. This is consistent with a mastery motivational climate (Ames, 1992), which aims to foster a learning environment where success is defined as effort and improvement, thus giving everyone equal opportunity to achieve success.

## Life skills development

An important aspect of the athletics challenges is to encourage the development of communication and interpersonal skills, decision-making, critical thinking and self-management behaviours (Mandigo et. al., 2008), which are highlighted on the challenge sheets. In order to facilitate the development of these skills, the following questions are provided for teachers to ask the students during or at the end of the lessons, as and when they see fit. It is suggested that teachers select which life skills they want to focus on in each lesson, in order to avoid too much repetition. The aim is for the teacher to facilitate student thought and discussions about the importance of these skills in developing physically active and positive lifestyles. The following list of possible questions is not intended to be prescriptive or exhaustive, but rather a stimulus for teachers to facilitate the development of these important life skills during athletics lessons.

### *Communication and interpersonal skills*

- How did you communicate with others in your group?
- Did others in your group encourage you?
- Was it easier to do the challenge when others encouraged you? Why?
- Is it important not to criticise others when they are trying hard? Why?
- What different types of communication can you use to help others?
- Why is it important to be able to communicate in different ways in sport? In school? In life?
- What are positive ways we can communicate to friends and family when we are trying to express how we are feeling?
- When you compete as a team, why is it important not to blame others if you lose?

■ ■ ■ ■ ATHLETICS CHALLENGES SHEETS

# Athletics challenges score sheets

Name..................................................................................................................

Date...................................................................................................................

Event..................................................................................................................

| Challenge | Score 1 | Score 2 | Score 3 | Best score |
|---|---|---|---|---|
|  |  |  |  |  |
|  |  |  |  |  |
|  |  |  |  |  |
|  |  |  |  |  |
|  |  |  |  |  |

Self-rated effort (1–10) ...................... Self-rated improvement (1–10) ..............

✂------------------------------------------------------------------------

# Athletics challenges score sheets

Name..................................................................................................................

Date...................................................................................................................

Event..................................................................................................................

| Challenge | Score 1 | Score 2 | Score 3 | Best score |
|---|---|---|---|---|
|  |  |  |  |  |
|  |  |  |  |  |
|  |  |  |  |  |
|  |  |  |  |  |
|  |  |  |  |  |

Self-rated effort (1–10) ...................... Self-rated improvement (1–10) ..............

**Figure 3** Athletics challenges score sheets

## ATHLETICS CHALLENGES ■ ■ ■ ■

### *Decision-making and critical thinking*

- Do you feel you made the best choices you were offered in the challenge? E.g. the distances between the cones, the pace you ran at, or the number of repetitions?
- What helped you to make these choices?
- When making choices and setting personal goals, why is it important that they are realistic and achievable? In sport? In school? At home?
- Why is it important to keep re-evaluating and setting new goals?
- In order to lead a physically active life, what sorts of choices do you have to make?
- In order to do well in your school work, what sorts of choices do you have to make?
- Why is it sometimes difficult to make these choices in sport, school or life?

### *Self-management skills*

- Did this practice challenge you?
- Why is it important to be challenged in sport, and in life?
- Do you prefer challenges against yourself or against others? Why?
- How do you feel if the challenge is too difficult to overcome?
- Is it important to never give up?
- Is there ever a time when we should give up and re-evaluate our goals?
- Is it easier to overcome difficult challenges if you have support from your friends or family?
- What sorts of challenges do you face in sport, in school, or at home?
- To be physically active, how important is it to be good at self-managing your free time?
- Do you think that you manage your time well to have a physically active lifestyle?
- What other things stop you from being more physically active?
- How much time per day do you think you should be physically active?
- Is it OK to cheat to win? Why? Why not?

## Team challenges

A co-operative reward structure is one where there is a positive interdependence amongst a group of students. In team challenges all of the group members work co-operatively to produce the best overall team score for a range of athletics challenges. Such team activities can help motivate students and encourage them to work hard for each other in order to achieve the best team score. Communication and interpersonal skills are particularly relevant in such team challenges and it is important for the teachers to emphasise these and to ask the relevant questions listed above. The following are examples of a team challenge circuit (see Figure 4) and scoring sheet. The actual challenges are purposely left open for the teacher to choose the most appropriate ones for the class, space and equipment available. Actual throwing implements such as shot and javelins should not be used in this type of lesson for safety reasons. Teams can compete against themselves to improve their own team scores, or against other teams in a competition. In the latter situation it is important that the teacher emphasises team cohesion following failure, and equal effort and input from all team members. Such team-challenge circuits can be organised as indoor or outdoor lessons.

■ ■ ■ ■ ATHLETICS CHALLENGES SHEETS

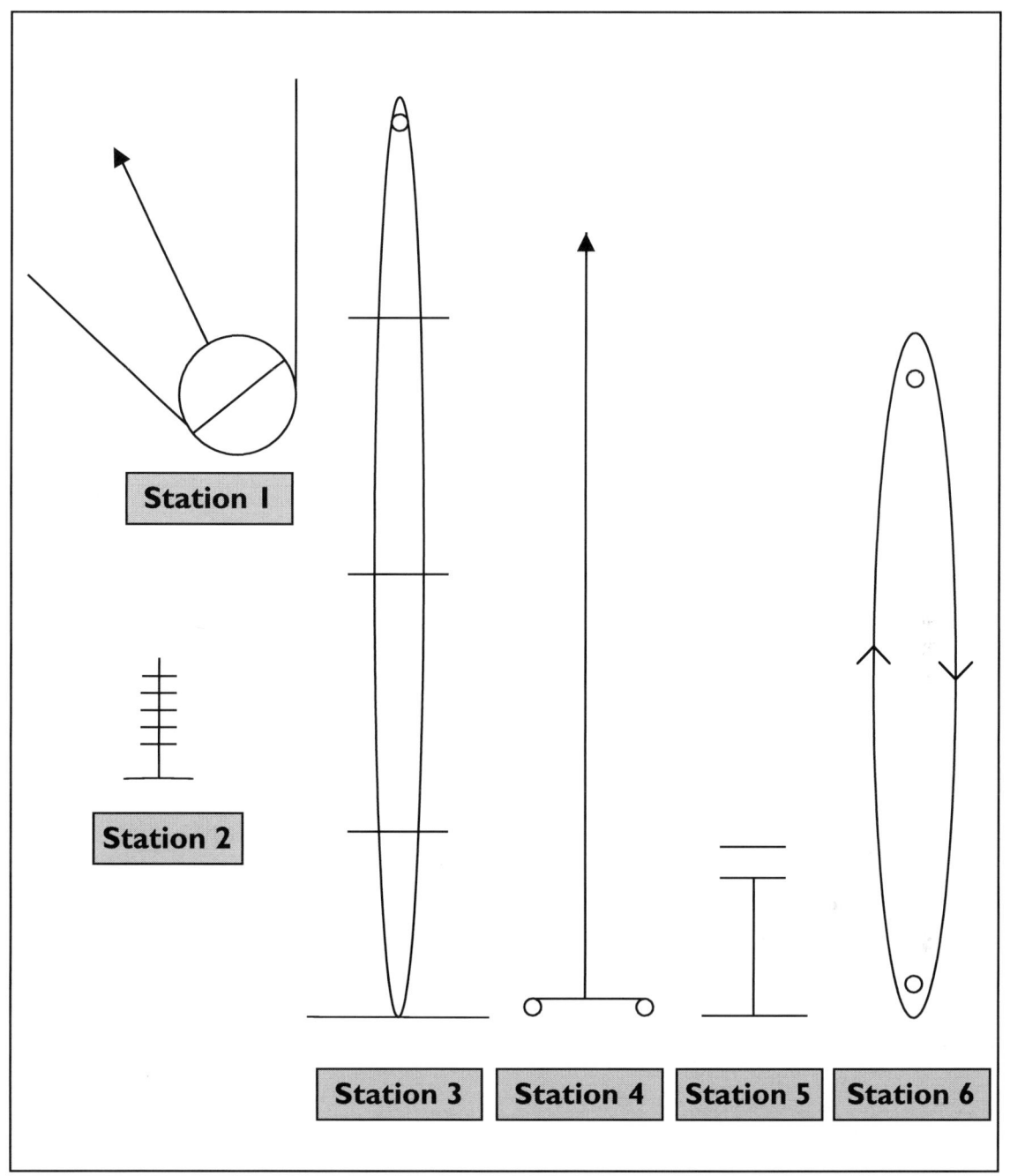

**Station 1** Shot put challenge
**Station 2** Triple jump challenge
**Station 3** Sprint hurdle challenge
**Station 4** Javelin challenge
**Station 5** Long jump challenge
**Station 6** Sprint challenge

**Figure 4** Team-challenge circuit example

ATHLETICS CHALLENGES ■ ■ ■ ■

# Team scoring sheet

Team number ..................................................................................................

| Challenge | Time / Dist. 1 | Time / Dist. 2 | Time / Dist. 3 | Time / Dist. 4 | Time / Dist. 5 | Time / Dist. 6 | Average time/ distance |
|---|---|---|---|---|---|---|---|
|  |  |  |  |  |  |  |  |
|  |  |  |  |  |  |  |  |
|  |  |  |  |  |  |  |  |
|  |  |  |  |  |  |  |  |
|  |  |  |  |  |  |  |  |
|  |  |  |  |  |  |  |  |

| Challenge | Team score ||||||  Position/points ||||||
|---|---|---|---|---|---|---|---|---|---|---|---|---|
|  | T1 | T2 | T3 | T4 | T5 | T6 | T1 | T2 | T3 | T4 | T5 | T6 |
|  |  |  |  |  |  |  |  |  |  |  |  |  |
|  |  |  |  |  |  |  |  |  |  |  |  |  |
|  |  |  |  |  |  |  |  |  |  |  |  |  |
|  |  |  |  |  |  |  |  |  |  |  |  |  |
|  |  |  |  |  |  |  |  |  |  |  |  |  |
|  |  |  |  |  |  |  |  |  |  |  |  |  |
| Totals |  |  |  |  |  |  |  |  |  |  |  |  |

**Points: 1st = 12; 2nd = 10; 3rd = 8; 4th = 6; 5th = 4; 6th = 2**

# ■ ■ ■ Sprinting 1 ■ ■ ■

### ■ *Equipment*

2 cones, stopwatch

### ■ *Challenge*

- Place 2 cones 5, 10 or 15m apart (choose your distance)
- Ask someone to time how long it takes you to run 4, 6 or 8 times (choose how many) between the cones
- Following a recovery, make further attempts to try to beat your personal best time
- Record your best time as a future target to improve upon

### ■ *Technique tips*

- Use a standing start with one foot ahead of the other
- Place your arms in the sprinting position with one forwards and one backwards, opposite to your legs
- Bend your knees to get into a low starting position
- Drive hard off your front foot on 'Go!'
- Pump your arms forwards and backwards powerfully
- Stay low during the sprints and on the turns

© 2011 Kevin Morgan, *Athletics Challenges*, Routledge.

## ■ Health and safety

- Warm-up correctly before starting to sprint (see warm-ups section)
- Ensure that the running area is flat, dry and not slippery
- Start to turn your body around just before you reach the cones to avoid twisting your knees
- Practise turning at a slower than sprinting pace before starting the challenge

## ■ Life skills

### Communication and interpersonal

- Communicate in a co-operative and friendly manner with others
- Encourage others to challenge themselves and achieve the best time they can
- Give others positive and constructive feedback on their effort and technique

### Decision-making and critical thinking

- Choose the best distance between the cones and number of repetitions to challenge yourself
- Set yourself realistic and achievable goals
- Keep re-evaluating and setting new goals

### Self-management

- Set up the challenge quickly and efficiently
- Challenge yourself to your maximum ability
- Focus on improving your own personal best
- Don't give up or cheat if the challenge gets difficult
- Maximise your activity time, allowing enough time to recover between attempts

© 2011 Kevin Morgan, *Athletics Challenges*, Routledge.

# ■ ■ ■ Sprinting 2 ■ ■ ■

### ■ Equipment

4–8 tennis balls/bean bags, 4–8 cones, stopwatch, tape measure (optional)

### ■ Challenge

- Place 4, 6 or 8 cones (choose how many) in a straight line, 2m apart
- Place an object (tennis ball or bean bag) beside each of the cones, except for the first one
- Using the first cone as a starting mark, run as quickly as you can, picking up each object in turn and placing it behind the starting cone
- Ask someone to time how long it takes you to pick up and return all the objects
- Following a recovery, make further attempts to try to beat your personal best time
- Record your best time as a future target to improve upon

### ■ Technique tips

- Adopt a standing start with one foot ahead of the other
- Place your arms in the sprinting position with one forwards and one backwards, opposite to your legs
- Bend your knees to get into a low starting position
- Drive hard off your front foot on 'Go!'
- Pump your arms forwards and backwards powerfully
- Stay low during the sprints and on the turns

## ■ Health and safety

- Warm-up correctly before starting to sprint (see warm-ups section)
- Ensure that the running area is flat, dry and not slippery
- Start to turn your body around just before you reach the cones to avoid twisting your knees
- Practise turning and collecting the objects at a slower-than-sprinting pace before starting the challenge

## ■ Life skills

### Communication and interpersonal

- Communicate in a co-operative and friendly manner with others
- Encourage others to challenge themselves and achieve the best time they can
- Give others positive and constructive feedback on their effort and technique

### Decision-making and critical thinking

- Choose the best number of cones to challenge yourself
- Set yourself realistic and achievable goals
- Keep re-evaluating and setting new goals

### Self-management

- Set up the challenge quickly and efficiently
- Challenge yourself to your maximum ability
- Focus on improving your own personal best
- Don't give up or cheat if the challenge gets difficult
- Maximise your activity time, allowing enough time to recover between attempts

© 2011 Kevin Morgan, *Athletics Challenges*, Routledge.

# ■ ■ ■ Sprinting 3 ■ ■ ■

### ▀▬ Equipment

2 cones, stopwatch, tape measure (optional)

### ▀▬ Challenge

- Place one cone as a starting mark
- Using a standing start, ask someone to time 3, 4 or 5 seconds (choose your time) by shouting 'Go!' and 'Stop!'
- See how far you can run in your chosen time
- Ask another person to place a cone at the point you got to in your chosen time
- Following a recovery, make further attempts to try to increase your distance
- Measure and record your best distance as a future target to improve upon

### ▀▬ Technique tips

- Adopt a standing start with one foot ahead of the other
- Place your arms in the sprinting position with one forwards and one backwards, opposite to your legs
- Bend your knees to get into a low starting position
- Drive hard off your front foot on 'Go!'
- Pump your arms forwards and backwards powerfully
- Keep sprinting until you hear 'Stop!'

## Health and safety

- Warm-up correctly before starting to sprint (see warm-ups section)
- Ensure that the running area is not slippery
- Do not run across the path of others
- Allow plenty of space to slow down without running into a wall or obstacle

## Life skills

### Communication and interpersonal

- Communicate in a co-operative and friendly manner with others
- Encourage others to challenge themselves and achieve the best distance they can
- Give others positive and constructive feedback on their effort and technique

### Decision-making and critical thinking

- Choose the best time to challenge yourself
- Set yourself realistic and achievable goals
- Keep re-evaluating and setting new goals

### Self-management

- Set up the challenge quickly and efficiently
- Challenge yourself to your maximum ability
- Focus on improving your own personal best
- Don't give up or cheat if the challenge gets difficult
- Maximise your activity time, allowing enough time to recover between attempts

© 2011 Kevin Morgan, *Athletics Challenges*, Routledge.

# ■ ■ ■ Sprinting 4 ■ ■ ■

### ▰ Equipment

2 cones, stopwatch, tape measure (optional)

### ▰ Challenge

- Place one cone as a starting mark
- Place another cone at a distance that you think you can get to; touch and return to the starting mark in 6, 8 or 10 seconds (choose your time)
- Ask someone to start you by saying 'Go!' and shouting 'Stop!' when your chosen time is up
- On 'Go!', sprint to the cone you placed, touch it and return before the time is up
- Following a recovery, make further attempts to try to move the cone further away
- Measure and record your best distance as a future target to improve upon

### ▰ Technique tips

- Adopt a standing start with one foot ahead of the other
- Place your arms in the sprinting position with one forwards and one backwards, opposite to your legs
- Bend your knees to get into a low starting position
- Drive hard off your front foot on 'Go!'
- Pump your arms forwards and backwards powerfully
- Stay low during the sprint and on the turn
- Keep sprinting until you hear 'Stop!'

© 2011 Kevin Morgan, *Athletics Challenges*, Routledge.

## ■ Health and safety

- Warm-up correctly before starting to sprint (see warm-ups section)
- Ensure that the running area is not slippery
- Do not run across the path of others
- Start to turn your body around just before you reach the cone to avoid twisting your knees
- Practise turning and collecting the cone at a slower-than-sprinting pace before starting the challenge
- Allow plenty of space to slow down without running into a wall or obstacle

## ■ Life skills

### Communication and interpersonal

- Communicate in a co-operative and friendly manner with others
- Encourage others to challenge themselves and achieve the best distance they can
- Give others positive and constructive feedback on their effort and technique

### Decision-making and critical thinking

- Choose the best time and distance to challenge yourself
- Set yourself realistic and achievable goals
- Keep re-evaluating and setting new goals

### Self-management

- Set up the challenge quickly and efficiently
- Challenge yourself to your maximum ability
- Focus on improving your own personal best
- Don't give up if the challenge gets difficult
- Maximise your activity time and allow enough time to recover between attempts

# Sprinting 5

## ▰▰▰ Equipment

2 cones, tape measure (optional)

## ▰▰▰ Challenge

- Work in pairs and place 2 cones 10, 15 or 20m apart (choose your distance)
- Working side-by-side with your partner, use one cone as a staring mark and perform any of the following starts to try to reach the other cone first:
  - lying on your front, with your head pointing towards the direction you are running
  - lying on your back, with your head pointing towards the direction you are running
  - sitting with your legs straight, facing away from the direction you are running
  - on your hands and knees, facing the direction you are running
  - standing with an upright posture, both feet together, arms by your sides, facing the direction you are running
  - adopting a standing start, one foot ahead of the other, a low body position and arms positioned opposite to your legs
  - adopting your own starting variations
- You can choose the same or a different start to your partner
- Take it in turns to choose the starts, and allow the person who doesn't choose to say 'Go!'
- Try to make it an even race where you are both challenged to your maximum

## ▰▰▰ Technique tips

- Wait for 'Go!' before starting to run
- React quickly and try to get into your running as soon as you can
- Keep your body low and push hard off the ground to pick up speed quickly
- Keep sprinting all the way to the cone

© 2011 Kevin Morgan, *Athletics Challenges*, Routledge.

## ■ Health and safety

- Warm-up correctly before starting to sprint (see warm-ups section)
- Ensure that the running area is flat, dry and not slippery
- When turning around before sprinting (e.g. lying on your back or sitting), make sure you have enough space between you and your partner so that you don't clash heads
- You **must** run in a straight line at all times
- Do not run across the path of others
- Allow plenty of space to slow down without running into a wall or obstacle

## ■ Life skills

### Communication and interpersonal

- Communicate with your partner in a co-operative and friendly manner
- Encourage each other to challenge yourselves
- Give others positive and constructive feedback on their effort and technique

### Decision-making and critical thinking

- Choose the best starts to challenge yourself and your partner
- Set yourself realistic and achievable goals
- Keep re-evaluating and setting new goals

### Self-management

- Set up the challenge quickly and efficiently
- Challenge yourself to your maximum ability
- Don't give up or cheat if the challenge gets difficult
- Maximise your activity time and allow enough time to recover between attempts

© 2011 Kevin Morgan, *Athletics Challenges*, Routledge.

# Sprinting 6

### ■■■ Equipment

3 cones, tape measure (optional)

### ■■■ Challenge

- Work in pairs and place a cone on the line between two running lanes
- Measure 20, 30 or 40m (choose your distance) in each direction away from the cone and your partner
- Place another cone and stand facing your partner, in different lanes, as shown below

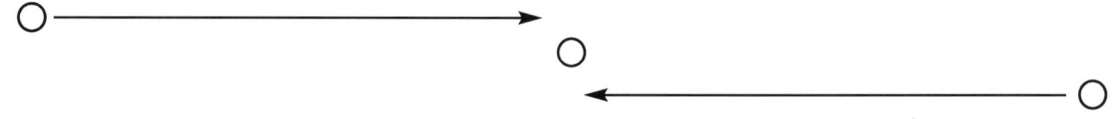

- On the signal from one of you, sprint in your own lane to try to get to the cone before, or at the same time as, your partner (decide if you want to race or pace each other)
- When you pass the central cone, slow down gradually until you reach the other starting cone
- Following a recovery, make further attempts, whilst adjusting the distances so that both of you are sprinting as fast as you can

### ■■■ Technique tips

- Adopt a standing start with one foot ahead of the other
- Place your arms in the sprinting position with one forwards and one backwards, opposite to your legs
- Bend your knees to get into a low starting position
- Drive hard off your front foot on 'Go!'
- Pump your arms forwards and backwards powerfully
- Stay low for the first part of the sprint until you reach full speed
- At full speed, your posture should be upright and your neck and shoulders relaxed
- Pick up your knees and drive off each leg powerfully

© 2011 Kevin Morgan, *Athletics Challenges*, Routledge.

## ■ Health and safety

- Warm-up correctly before starting to sprint (see warm-ups section)
- Do not run in the same lane as your partner
- Allow plenty of space to slow down without running into a wall or obstacle

## ■ Life skills

### Communication and interpersonal

- Communicate with your partner in a co-operative and friendly manner
- Encourage each other to challenge yourselves
- Give each other positive and constructive feedback on your effort and technique

### Decision-making and critical thinking

- Choose the best distance to challenge yourself and your partner
- Set yourself realistic and achievable goals
- Keep re-evaluating and setting new goals

### Self-management

- Set up the challenge quickly and efficiently
- Challenge yourself to your maximum ability
- Don't give up or cheat if the challenge gets difficult
- Maximise your activity time and allow enough time to recover between attempts

# Sustained running 1

### ■ Equipment

8 cones, stopwatch, whistle (optional)

### ■ Challenge

- Place a cone every 50m around the track/running area
- Position yourself by one of the cones ready to start running
- On the whistle, start running at a pace you think you can continue at for 2, 3 or 4 minutes (choose your time)
- Ask someone to say 'Go!' and to time 2, 3 or 4 minutes, shouting 'Stop!' or blowing a whistle when the time is up
- Stop running when the time is up and work out how far you have run in your chosen time
- Record your best distance as a future target to improve upon

### ■ Technique tips

- Set off at a sensible and steady pace
- Run with an upright posture
- Keep your head still and look straight ahead
- Relax your head, neck, arms and shoulders
- Bend your arms to about 90 degrees at the elbow
- Gently swing your arms forwards and backwards and slightly across your body
- Run with a natural, easy stride length
- Push off the ground to extend your leg fully on each stride
- Run with a fairly low knee lift to conserve energy on each stride

© 2011 Kevin Morgan, *Athletics Challenges*, Routledge.

## ▰ Health and safety

- Warm-up correctly before starting to run (see warm-ups section)
- Do not run across the path of others
- Overtake on the outside of other runners
- Walk at a fast pace if you cannot sustain the running

## ▰ Life skills

### Communication and interpersonal

- Communicate in a co-operative and friendly manner with others
- Encourage others to challenge themselves and achieve the best time they can
- Give others positive and constructive feedback on their effort and technique

### Decision-making and critical thinking

- Choose the best time to challenge yourself
- Set yourself realistic and achievable goals
- Keep re-evaluating and setting new goals

### Self-management

- Set up the challenge quickly and efficiently
- Challenge yourself to your maximum ability
- Focus on improving your own personal best
- Don't give up or cheat if the challenge gets difficult

# Sustained running 2

## ■ Equipment

8 cones, stopwatch

## ■ Challenge

- Place a cone every 50m around the track/running area
- Run 50m at a pace you think you could continue for 800m (choose your pace)
- Extend this distance to 400m, checking the time every 50m around the track (marked out with cones)
- Work out how long it would take you to run 400, 600 or 800m at this pace (choose your distance)
- Run your chosen distance without using the stopwatch and ask someone to time it for you
- Compare your actual time with your predicted time
- Record your time as a future target to improve upon

## ■ Technique tips

- Set off at a sensible and steady pace
- Run with an upright posture
- Keep your head still and look straight ahead
- Relax your head, neck, arms and shoulders
- Bend your arms to about 90 degrees at the elbow
- Gently swing your arms forwards and backwards and slightly across your body
- Run with a natural, easy stride length
- Push off the ground to extend your leg fully on each stride

© 2011 Kevin Morgan, *Athletics Challenges*, Routledge.

## ■ Health and safety

- Warm-up correctly before starting to run (see warm-ups section)
- Do not run across the path of others
- Overtake on the outside of other runners
- Walk at a fast pace if you cannot sustain the running

## ■ Life skills

### Communication and interpersonal

- Communicate in a co-operative and friendly manner with others
- Encourage others to challenge themselves and achieve the best time they can
- Give others positive and constructive feedback on their effort and technique

### Decision-making and critical thinking

- Choose the best distance to challenge yourself
- Set yourself realistic and achievable goals
- Keep re-evaluating and setting new goals

### Self-management

- Set up the challenge quickly and efficiently
- Challenge yourself to your maximum ability
- Focus on improving your own personal best
- Don't give up or cheat if the challenge gets difficult

# Sustained running 3

### ■ Equipment

Stopwatch

### ■ Challenge

- In groups, run a combined distance of 800 or 1500m (choose your distance) to achieve your fastest group time
- Set a minimum and maximum distance for each runner and decide how far each group member will run
- Compare your team time with the class/school/national/world record for your chosen distance
- Following a recovery, make further attempts to try to improve your team time
- Record your best time as a future target to improve upon

### ■ Technique tips

- Run with an upright posture
- Keep your head still and look straight ahead
- Relax your head, neck, arms and shoulders
- Bend your arms to about 90 degrees at the elbow
- Push off the ground to extend your leg fully on each stride

## Health and safety

- Warm-up correctly before starting to run (see warm-ups section)
- Do not run across the path of others

## Life skills

### Communication and interpersonal

- Communicate in a co-operative and friendly manner with others in your group
- Encourage each other to achieve the best group time
- Give others positive and constructive feedback on their effort and technique

### Decision-making and critical thinking

- Choose the best distance, as a group and individually, to challenge yourself
- Set yourself realistic and achievable goals
- Keep re-evaluating and setting new goals

### Self-management

- Challenge yourself to your maximum ability
- Focus on improving your own personal and group best
- Don't give up or cheat if the challenge gets difficult

# Sustained running 4

### ■ Equipment

4–6 cones, stopwatch

### ■ Challenge

- Work in groups of approximately 4–6 and number yourselves starting from 1
- Number 1 runs for a set time, e.g. 1 minute (choose your times, which can be different for each runner)
- The next runner in the team marks how far number 1 has run with a cone and then starts from that mark for his/her run
- Continue this process until all the students in the group have run
- Calculate the overall distance that the group has run
- Following a recovery, make further attempts to try to improve your team distance
- Record the individual times and best group distance as a future target to improve upon

### ■ Technique tips

- Run with an upright posture
- Keep your head still and look straight ahead
- Relax your head, neck, arms and shoulders
- Bend your arms to about 90 degrees at the elbow
- Gently swing your arms forwards and backwards and slightly across your body
- Run with a natural, easy stride length
- Push off the ground to extend your leg fully on each stride
- Run with a fairly low knee lift to conserve energy on each stride

© 2011 Kevin Morgan, *Athletics Challenges*, Routledge.

## Health and safety

- Warm-up correctly before starting to run (see warm-ups section)
- Do not run across the path of others

## Life skills

### Communication and interpersonal

- Communicate in a co-operative and friendly manner with others in your group
- Encourage each other to achieve the best group distance
- Give others positive and constructive feedback on their effort and technique

### Decision-making and critical thinking

- Choose the best times, as a group and individually, to challenge yourselves
- Set yourself realistic and achievable goals
- Keep re-evaluating and setting new goals

### Self-management

- Challenge yourself to your maximum ability
- Focus on improving your own personal and group best
- Don't give up or cheat if the challenge gets difficult

# Sustained running 5

### ■ Equipment

10 cones, stopwatch

### ■ Challenge

- Work in groups of 4, of similar sustained running ability, and number yourselves 1–4
- Place a cone every 50m around the track/running area and another 2 cones, 50m apart, in the centre or to the side of the track/running area
- Number 1 runs a lap of the track (choose your pace)
- Starting at the same time as Number 1, Numbers 2–4 run 50m shuttles in turn at the same pace as number 1
- Watch number 1 to maintain the same pace by completing each shuttle at the same time as he/she gets to a cone
- At the end of number 1's lap, change the runner immediately so that everyone has a go at the full lap without the shuttle runs stopping
- Record the overall group time for the 4 laps as a future target to improve upon

### ■ Technique tips

- Set off at a sensible and steady pace
- Run with an upright posture
- Keep your head still and look straight ahead
- Relax your head, neck, arms and shoulders
- Bend your arms to about 90 degrees at the elbow
- Gently swing your arms forwards and backwards and slightly across your body
- Run with a natural, easy stride length
- Push off the ground to extend your leg fully on each stride
- Run with a fairly low knee lift to conserve energy on each stride

© 2011 Kevin Morgan, *Athletics Challenges*, Routledge.

## Health and safety

- Warm-up correctly before starting to run (see warm-ups section)
- Do not run across the path of others

## Life skills

### Communication and interpersonal

- Communicate in a co-operative and friendly manner with others in your group
- Encourage each other to achieve the best group time
- Give others positive and constructive feedback on their effort and technique

### Decision-making and critical thinking

- Choose the best pace, as a group and individually, to challenge yourselves
- Set yourself realistic and achievable goals
- Keep re-evaluating and setting new goals

### Self-management

- Challenge yourself to your maximum ability
- Focus on improving your own personal and group best
- Don't give up or cheat if the challenge gets difficult

# Sustained running 6

### ■ Equipment

Approx. 10–15 cones/bean bags per group, stopwatch, 3 plastic hoops (optional)

### ■ Challenge

- Work in groups of 4–6
- Collect 12 cones/bean bags for your group (a different colour for each group if more than one group is doing the challenge at the same time)
- Ask someone to say 'Go!'
- On 'Go!', each group member takes it in turns to run and place a cone/bean bag in a scoring zone on the track (e.g. 100m and back = 10 points, 150m and back = 20 points, 200m and back = 50 points)
- The team continues for a set time, e.g. 5 minutes (choose your time but if longer than 5 minutes more cones/bean bags may be needed)
- Add up the total team points and record it as a future target to improve upon

### ■ Technique tips

- Set off at a sensible and steady pace
- Run with an upright posture
- Keep your head still and look straight ahead
- Relax your head, neck, arms and shoulders
- Bend your arms to about 90 degrees at the elbow
- Gently swing your arms forwards and backwards and slightly across your body
- Run with a natural, easy stride length
- Push off the ground to extend your leg fully on each stride
- Run with a fairly low knee lift to conserve energy on each stride

© 2011 Kevin Morgan, *Athletics Challenges*, Routledge.

## ▬ Health and safety

- Warm-up correctly before starting to run (see warm-ups section)
- Do not run across the path of others

## ▬ Life skills

### Communication and interpersonal

- Communicate in a co-operative and friendly manner with others in your group
- Encourage each other to achieve the best group score
- Give others positive and constructive feedback on their effort and technique

### Decision-making and critical thinking

- Choose the best distances, as a group and individually, to challenge yourselves
- Set yourself realistic and achievable goals
- Keep re-evaluating and setting new goals

### Self-management

- Challenge yourself to your maximum ability
- Focus on improving your own personal and group best
- Don't give up or cheat if the challenge gets difficult

# Hurdling 1

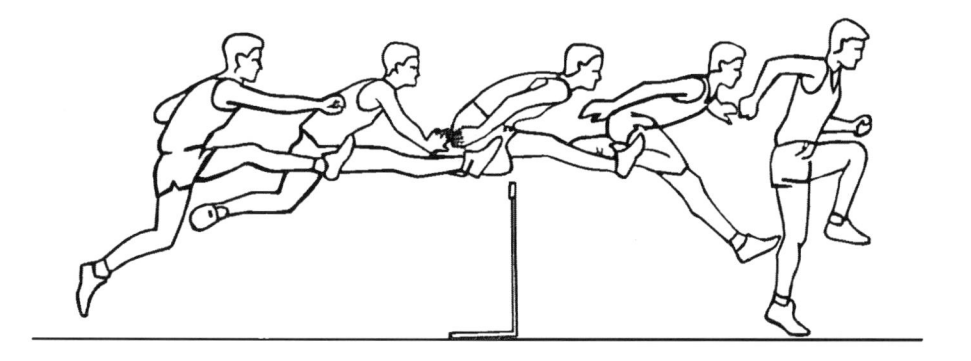

### ■ Equipment

5 cones, stopwatch, tape measure (optional), 4 two-way or foam wedge/plastic hurdles (if available)

### ■ Challenge

- Place a cone as a starting mark, another cone 10m ahead of it and 3 more cones 5, 6 or 7m apart (choose your distance)
- Practise running over the cones to find out which leg you prefer to go over the cone first
- Run as fast as you can over the cones, trying to get the same leg going over first each time
- Ask someone to time how long it takes you to run over all the cones
- Following a recovery, make further attempts to try to beat your personal best time
- Record your best time as a future target to improve upon
- Progress to two-way or foam wedge/plastic hurdles

### ■ Technique tips

- Choose a distance between the cones that allows you to use 3 full running strides between them
- Try to lead with the same leg each time over the cones
- After your leading leg touches the ground over each cone, try counting the rhythm '1, 2, 3, over'
- Think of running over the cones, rather than jumping

## ▰ Health and safety

- Warm-up correctly before starting to hurdle (see warm-ups section)
- Ensure that the running area is flat, dry and not slippery
- Do not cross the path of other runners
- Allow plenty of space to slow down at the end without running into a wall or obstacle

## ▰ Life skills

### Communication and interpersonal

- Communicate in a co-operative and friendly manner with others
- Encourage others to challenge themselves and achieve the best time they can
- Give others positive and constructive feedback on their effort and technique

### Decision-making and critical thinking

- Choose the best distances between cones/hurdles to challenge yourself
- Set yourself realistic and achievable goals
- Keep re-evaluating and setting new goals

### Self-management

- Challenge yourself to your maximum ability
- Focus on improving your own personal best
- Don't give up or cheat if the challenge gets difficult

# Hurdling 2

## ■ Equipment

5 cones, stopwatch, tape measure (optional), 4 two-way or foam wedge/plastic hurdles (if available)

## ■ Challenge

- Place a cone as a starting mark, another cone 10m ahead of it and 3 more cones 6, 7 or 8m apart (choose your distance)
- Run as fast as you can over the cones, trying to get alternate legs going over first each time (i.e. right-left-right-left)
- Ask someone to time how long it takes you to run over all the cones
- Following a recovery, make further attempts to try to beat your personal best time
- Record your best time as a future target to improve upon
- Progress to two-way or foam wedge/plastic hurdles

## ■ Technique tips

- Choose a distance between the cones that allows you to use 4 full running strides between them
- Try to lead with a different leg each time over the cones i.e. right-left-right-left
- After your leading leg touches the ground over each cone, try counting the rhythm '1, 2, 3, 4 over'
- Think of running over the cones, rather than jumping

## ■ *Health and safety*

- Warm-up correctly before starting to hurdle (see warm-ups section)
- Ensure that the running area is flat, dry and not slippery
- Do not cross the path of other runners
- Allow plenty of space to slow down at the end without running into a wall or obstacle

## ■ *Life skills*

### Communication and interpersonal

- Communicate in a co-operative and friendly manner with others
- Encourage others to challenge themselves and achieve the best time they can
- Give others positive and constructive feedback on their effort and technique

### Decision-making and critical thinking

- Choose the best distances between cones/hurdles to challenge yourself
- Set yourself realistic and achievable goals
- Keep re-evaluating and setting new goals

### Self-management

- Challenge yourself to your maximum ability
- Focus on improving your own personal best
- Don't give up or cheat if the challenge gets difficult

# Hurdling 3

### ■■■ Equipment

1 cone, 4 hurdles (two-way or foam wedge/plastic hurdles, if available), stopwatch, tape measure (optional)

### ■■■ Challenge

- Place a cone as a starting mark, a hurdle 10m ahead of it, 3 more hurdles 5, 6 or 7m apart (choose your distance between hurdles and their height) and a final cone another 10m ahead of the last hurdle
- Practise walking to the side of the hurdles (to the left if you prefer to lead with your right leg and vice versa) with only your leading leg going over the hurdle
- Build up the walk to a run and then a sprint
- Ask someone to time how long it takes you to run over all the hurdles
- Following a recovery, make further attempts to try to beat your personal best time
- Record your best time as a future target to improve upon

### ■■■ Technique tips

- Choose a distance between the hurdles that allows you to use 3 full running strides between them
- Try to lead with the same leg each time over the hurdles
- After your leading leg touches the ground over each hurdle, try counting the rhythm '1, 2, 3, over'
- Think of running over the hurdles, rather than jumping
- Pick your leading knee up quickly with a bent leg at the hurdles
- Kick your leading leg straight forwards over the hurdles, with your heel leading
- Try to get your leading leg back down to the ground quickly after each hurdle

© 2011 Kevin Morgan, *Athletics Challenges*, Routledge.

## ■ Health and safety

- Warm-up correctly before starting to hurdle (see warm-ups section)
- Ensure that the running area is flat, dry and not slippery
- Start by using two-way or foam wedge hurdles, if available, to build confidence and then progress to full hurdles if and when appropriate, whilst still having the choice of the safer equipment
- Do not cross the path of other runners
- Choose hurdle heights and distances between them that allow you to clear them comfortably without overstretching
- Allow plenty of space to slow down at the end without running into a wall or obstacle

## ■ Life skills

### Communication and interpersonal

- Communicate in a co-operative and friendly manner with others
- Encourage others to challenge themselves and achieve the best time they can
- Give others positive and constructive feedback on their effort and technique

### Decision-making and critical thinking

- Choose the best distances between, and height of, hurdles to challenge yourself
- Set yourself realistic and achievable goals
- Keep re-evaluating and setting new goals

### Self-management

- Challenge yourself to your maximum ability
- Focus on improving your own personal best
- Don't give up or cheat if the challenge gets difficult

# Hurdling 4

### ■■■ Equipment

2 cones, 4 hurdles (two-way or foam wedge/plastic hurdles, if available), stopwatch, tape measure (optional)

### ■■■ Challenge

- Place a cone as a starting mark, a hurdle 10m ahead of it, 3 more hurdles 5, 6 or 7m apart (choose your distance between hurdles and their height) and a final cone another 10m ahead of the last hurdle
- Practise walking to the side of the hurdles (to the right if you prefer to lead with your right leg and vice versa) with only your trailing leg going over the hurdle
- Build up the walk to a run and then a sprint
- Ask someone to time how long it takes you to run over all the hurdles
- Following a recovery, make further attempts to try to beat your personal best time
- Record your best time as a future target to improve upon

### ■■■ Technique tips

- Choose a distance between the hurdles that allows you to use 3 full running strides between them
- Try to use the same trailing leg each time over the hurdles
- After your leading leg touches the ground to the side of the hurdle, try counting the rhythm '1, 2, 3, over'
- Think of running over the hurdles, rather than jumping
- Place your leading leg beyond the hurdle before pulling the trailing leg through
- Push the knee of your trailing leg forward, with the knee bent and the ankle tucked in
- Swing the knee of the trailing leg to the side of your body and back into the line of running

© 2011 Kevin Morgan, *Athletics Challenges*, Routledge.

## ■ Health and safety

- Warm-up correctly before starting to hurdle (see warm-ups section)
- Ensure that the running area is flat, dry and not slippery
- Start by using two-way or foam wedge hurdles, if available, to build confidence and then progress to full hurdles if and when appropriate, whilst still having the choice of the safer equipment
- Do not cross the path of other runners
- Choose hurdle heights and distances between them that allow you to clear them comfortably without overstretching
- Allow plenty of space to slow down at the end without running into a wall or obstacle

## ■ Life skills

### Communication and interpersonal

- Communicate in a co-operative and friendly manner with others
- Encourage others to challenge themselves and achieve the best time they can
- Give others positive and constructive feedback on their effort and technique

### Decision-making and critical thinking

- Choose the best distances between and height of hurdles to challenge yourself
- Set yourself realistic and achievable goals
- Keep re-evaluating and setting new goals

### Self-management

- Challenge yourself to your maximum ability
- Focus on improving your own personal best
- Don't give up or cheat if the challenge gets difficult

© 2011 Kevin Morgan, *Athletics Challenges*, Routledge.

# Hurdling 5

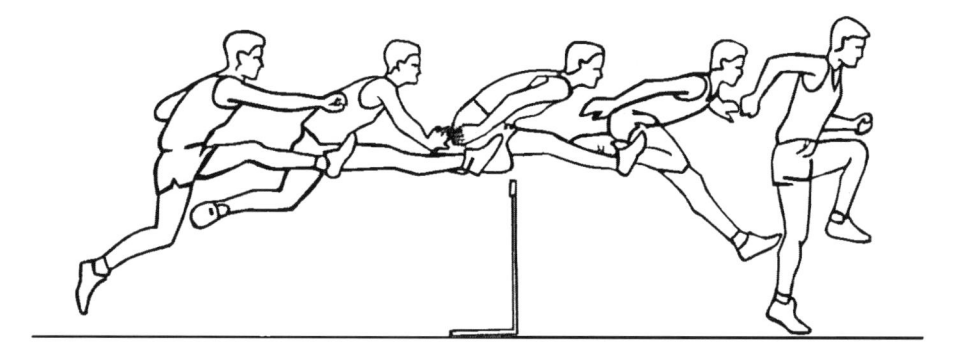

### ■■■ Equipment

1 cone, 4 hurdles (two-way or foam wedge/plastic hurdles, if available), stopwatch, tape measure (optional)

### ■■■ Challenge

- Place a cone as a starting mark, a hurdle 10m ahead of it, 3 more hurdles 5, 6 or 7m apart (choose your distance between hurdles and their height) and a final cone another 10m ahead of the last hurdle
- Run as fast as you can over the hurdles, trying to get the same leg going over first each time
- Ask someone to time how long it takes you to run over all the hurdles
- Following a recovery, have further attempts to try to beat your personal best time
- Record your best time as a future target to improve upon

### ■■■ Technique tips

- Choose a distance between the hurdles that allows you to use 3 full running strides between them
- Try to lead with the same leg each time over the hurdles
- After your leading leg touches the ground over each hurdle, try counting the rhythm '1, 2, 3, over'
- Think of running over the hurdles, rather than jumping
- For the leading leg, think of picking your knee up quickly with a bent leg
- Kick the leading leg straight forwards over the hurdle, with your heel leading
- Try to get your leading leg back down to the ground quickly after each hurdle
- Push the knee of the trailing leg forward, with the knee bent and the ankle tucked in
- Swing the knee of the trailing leg to the side of your body and back into the line of running

© 2011 Kevin Morgan, *Athletics Challenges*, Routledge.

## ■ Health and safety

- Warm-up correctly before starting to run (see warm-ups section)
- Ensure that the running area is flat, dry and not slippery
- Start by using two-way or foam wedge hurdles, if available, to build confidence and then progress to full hurdles if and when appropriate, whilst still having the choice of the safer equipment
- Do not cross the path of other runners
- Choose hurdle heights and distances between them that allow you to clear them comfortably without overstretching
- Allow plenty of space to slow down at the end without running into a wall or obstacle

## ■ Life skills

### Communication and interpersonal

- Communicate in a co-operative and friendly manner with others
- Encourage others to challenge themselves and achieve the best time they can
- Give others positive and constructive feedback on their effort and technique

### Decision-making and critical thinking

- Choose the best distances between and height of hurdles to challenge yourself
- Set yourself realistic and achievable goals
- Keep re-evaluating and setting new goals

### Self-management

- Challenge yourself to your maximum ability
- Focus on improving your own personal best
- Don't give up or cheat if the challenge gets difficult

# ■ ■ ■ Hurdling 6 ■ ■ ■

## ■ Equipment

2 cones, 8 two-way or foam wedge/plastic hurdles, stopwatch, tape measure (optional)

## ■ Challenge

- Work in small groups of 4–6
- In running lane 1, place a cone as a starting mark, a two-way or foam hurdle 10 metre ahead of it, 3 more hurdles 5, 6 or 7m apart (choose your distance between hurdles and their height) and a final cone another 10m ahead of the last hurdle
- Set up the same equipment, in the same way, in lane 2, directly beside lane 1
- Split the group evenly so that half the group are standing in single-file in lane 1 and the other half in lane 2 at the other end of the hurdles facing the runners in lane 1
- Start with the first runner in lane 1 and run as fast as you can over the hurdles one at a time in a shuttle relay
- Touch the next person facing you on the shoulder to start them on their run
- Ask someone to time how long it takes the whole group to run over all the hurdles, or time it yourselves
- Following a recovery, make further attempts to try to beat your best group time
- Record your best time as a future target to improve upon

## ■ Technique tips

- Choose a distance between the hurdles that allows you to use 3 full running strides between them
- Try to lead with the same leg each time over the hurdles
- After your leading leg touches the ground over each hurdle, try counting the rhythm '1, 2, 3, over'
- Think of running over the hurdles, rather than jumping them
- For the leading leg, think of picking your knee up quickly with a bent leg
- Kick the leading leg straight forwards over the hurdle, with your heel leading
- Try to get your leading leg back down to the ground quickly after each hurdle
- Push the knee of the trailing leg forward, with the knee bent and the ankle tucked in
- Swing the knee of the trailing leg to the side of your body and back into the line of running

© 2011 Kevin Morgan, *Athletics Challenges*, Routledge.

## ■ Health and safety

- Warm-up correctly before starting to run (see warm-ups section)
- Ensure that the running area is flat, dry and not slippery
- Do not cross the path of other runners
- Choose hurdle heights and distances between them that allow you to clear them comfortably without overstretching
- Allow plenty of space to slow down at the end without running into a wall or obstacle

## ■ Life skills

### Communication and interpersonal

- Communicate in a co-operative and friendly manner with others
- Encourage others to challenge themselves to achieve the best team time
- Give others positive and constructive feedback on their effort and technique

### Decision-making and critical thinking

- Choose the best distances between and height of hurdles to challenge yourselves
- Set yourselves realistic and achievable goals
- Keep re-evaluating and setting new goals

### Self-management

- Challenge yourself to your maximum ability
- Focus on improving your own personal and group best
- Don't give up or cheat if the challenge gets difficult

# Relays 1

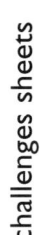

### ■ Equipment

1 relay baton, 2 cones, stopwatch, tape measure (optional)

### ■ Challenge

- Work in groups of 5
- Place one cone as a starting mark and a second cone 20m away
- Split the group into a 3 and a 2 and position yourselves with the group of 3 by cone 1 and the other two facing them by cone 2
- Decide on your running order and run a continuous shuttle relay for 1 minute, 90 seconds or 2 minutes (choose your time)
- Ask someone to time you and count the number of shuttles, or do this yourselves
- Following a recovery, make further attempts to try to improve your number of shuttles
- Record your best number as a future target to improve upon

### ■ Technique tips

- To exchange the baton, hold it up vertically in the last few strides and allow the next runner to grab the top or bottom half of the baton
- Wait until you get a good grip of the baton before starting to sprint

## ▮▮ Health and safety

- Warm-up correctly before starting to sprint (see warm-ups section)
- Leave enough space for each runner to run past the group safely
- Be careful not to push the baton into the hand of the next runner; just hold it up vertically to avoid any thumb injuries
- Do not run across the path of others

## ▮▮ Life skills

### Communication and interpersonal

- Communicate in a co-operative and friendly manner with others in your group
- Encourage each other to achieve the best group total you can
- Give each other positive and constructive feedback on your effort and technique

### Decision-making and critical thinking

- Choose the best time to challenge yourselves
- Set yourself realistic and achievable goals
- Keep re-evaluating and setting new goals

### Self-management

- Set up the challenge quickly and efficiently
- Challenge yourself to your maximum ability
- Don't give up or cheat if the challenge gets difficult
- Maximise your activity time and allow enough time to recover between attempts

# Relays 2

### ■ Equipment

4 cones, tape measure (optional), relay baton (optional)

### ■ Challenge

- Work in pairs and label yourselves A and B
- Place one cone as a starting mark, a second cone 10m ahead, a third cone 5m further ahead and a fourth cone 10, 15 or 20m away (choose your distance) as shown below

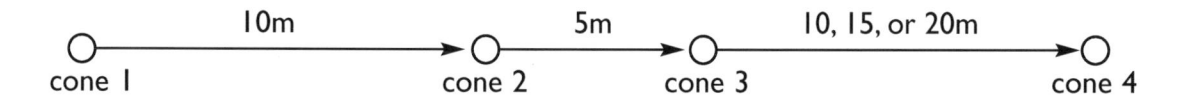

```
  ○ ——10m——→ ○ ——5m——→ ○ ——10, 15, or 20m——→ ○
cone 1          cone 2      cone 3                    cone 4
```

- Position yourselves at the starting mark with A standing next to cone 1 and B next to cone 3
- A sprints towards B (who is static at this time) and when he/she reaches cone 2, B sprints away towards cone 4
- A tries to touch B on the LEFT shoulder with his/her RIGHT hand before reaching cone 4
- Following a recovery, change positions and make further attempts, whilst adjusting the distances between cones 2 and 3, so that both of you are sprinting as fast as you can
- Progress to the incoming runner (the one who starts behind) calling 'hand' when he/she gets close enough to the outgoing runner (the one in front) and then touching the LEFT hand (palm up) with the RIGHT hand (palm down)
- Progress further to exchanging a relay baton from A to B

### ■ Technique tips

- Adopt a standing start with one foot ahead of the other
- Place your arms in the sprinting position with one forwards and one back, opposite to your legs
- Bend your knees to get into a low starting position
- Drive hard off your front foot on 'Go!'
- Pump your arms forwards and backwards powerfully
- Run in a straight line and once you start to run don't look back

© 2011 Kevin Morgan, *Athletics Challenges*, Routledge.

## ▮▮ Health and safety

- Warm-up correctly before starting to sprint (see warm-ups section)
- You **must** run in a straight line at all times
- The person behind should run to the left of the person in front and use his/her right hand to touch the left shoulder or hand of the person in front
- **Do not** run across the path of others
- Allow plenty of space to slow down without running into a wall or obstacles

## ▮▮ Life skills

### Communication and interpersonal

- Communicate in a co-operative and friendly manner with your partner
- Give each other positive and constructive feedback on your effort and technique

### Decision-making and critical thinking

- Choose the best time and distance to challenge yourself
- Set yourself realistic and achievable goals
- Keep re-evaluating and setting new goals

### Self-management

- Set up the challenge quickly and efficiently
- Challenge yourself to your maximum ability
- Don't give up or cheat if the challenge gets difficult
- Maximise your activity time and allow enough time to recover between attempts

# Relays 3

## ■ Equipment

1 relay baton, 4 cones, stopwatch, tape measure (optional)

## ■ Challenge

- Work in groups of 4
- Place one cone as a starting mark, a second cone 10m ahead, a third cone 20m further ahead and a fourth cone another 10m away, as shown below

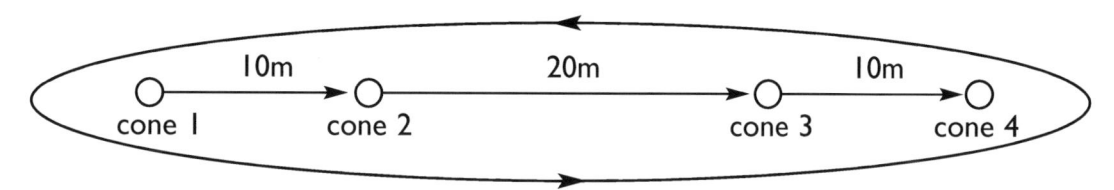

```
         10m              20m              10m
   O------------>O------------------>O------------>O
 cone 1        cone 2              cone 3        cone 4
```

- Decide on your running order and how you will exchange the baton
- Runner 1 starts and runs from cone 1, past cones 2 and 3, around cone 4 and back around cone 1
- Exchange the baton to the next group runner between cones 2 and 3
- Ask someone to start you and time how long it takes the whole team to complete 1 lap each
- Try different methods of exchanging the baton to try to improve your time
- Record your best time as a future target to improve upon

## ■ Technique tips

### UPSWEEP BATON EXCHANGE

**Outgoing runner**
- Present the palm of your receiving hand facing towards the incoming runner
- Form a 'V' between your fingers and thumb to receive the baton
- Keep your receiving arm straight and still at about hip height
- Grip the baton tightly and sprint away

**Incoming runner**
- Pass the baton with an upward-pushing motion into the outgoing runner's hand
- Place the nearest part of the baton firmly and as far as possible into the hand of the outgoing runner

## DOWNSWEEP BATON EXCHANGE

### Outgoing runner
- Present the palm of your receiving hand facing upwards and towards the incoming runner
- Form a 'V' between your fingers and thumb to receive the baton
- Keep your receiving arm straight and still at above hip height and near shoulder height
- Grip the baton tightly and sprint away

### Incoming runner
- Pass the baton with a downward, forward-pushing motion into the outgoing runner's hand
- Place the upper third (furthest part) of the baton firmly into the hand of the outgoing runner

## ■ Health and safety

- Warm-up correctly before starting to sprint (see warm-ups section)
- Leave enough space for each runner to run past the group safely
- The person behind (incoming runner) should run to the side of the person in front (outgoing runner) to avoid tripping him/her
- The outgoing runner should set off early enough to avoid the incoming runner running into him/her, or having to slow down suddenly
- Do not run across the path of others

## ■ Life skills

### Communication and interpersonal

- Communicate in a co-operative and friendly manner with others in your group
- Encourage each other to achieve the best group time you can
- Give each other positive and constructive feedback on your effort and technique

### Decision-making and critical thinking

- Set yourself realistic and achievable goals
- Keep re-evaluating and setting new goals

### Self-management

- Set up the challenge quickly and efficiently
- Challenge yourself to your maximum ability
- Don't give up or cheat if the challenge gets difficult
- Maximise your activity time and allow enough time to recover between attempts

# ■ ■ ■ Relays 4 ■ ■ ■

## ■ Equipment

1 relay baton, 8 cones, stopwatch, tape measure (optional)

## ■ Challenge

- Work in groups of 4
- Place a cone as a starting point at the of beginning of a 100m straight
- Measure 15m from the start to the first 'baton change' box
- Use 6 more cones to mark 3 x 15m 'baton change' boxes with a 15m gap between each
- Measure 10m from the end of the last 'baton change' box to the finish (100m in total, as shown below)

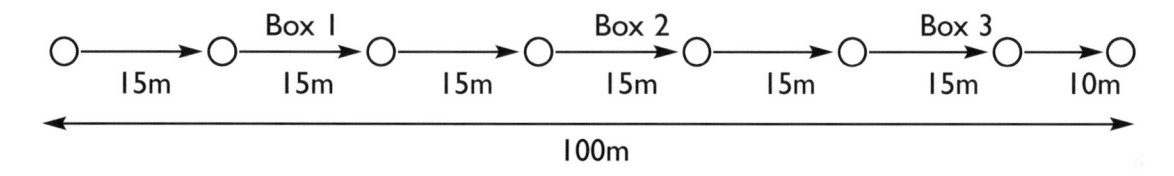

```
        Box 1          Box 2          Box 3
O─────▶O─────▶O─────▶O─────▶O─────▶O─────▶O─────▶O
  15m     15m    15m    15m    15m    15m    10m
◀─────────────────────── 100m ───────────────────────▶
```

- Decide on your running order and how you will exchange the baton
- Ask someone to start you and time how long it takes you to run the 100m as a group
- Try different methods of exchanging the baton to try to improve your time
- Record your best time as a future target to improve upon

## ■ Technique tips

### UPSWEEP BATON EXCHANGE

**Outgoing runner**
- Present the palm of your receiving hand facing towards the incoming runner
- Form a 'V' between your fingers and thumb to receive the baton
- Keep your receiving arm straight and still at about hip height
- Grip the baton tightly and sprint away

**Incoming runner**
- Pass the baton with an upward-pushing motion into the outgoing runner's hand
- Place the nearest part of the baton firmly and as far as possible into the hand of the outgoing runner

© 2011 Kevin Morgan, *Athletics Challenges*, Routledge.

## DOWNSWEEP BATON EXCHANGE

### Outgoing runner

- Present the palm of your receiving hand facing upwards and towards the incoming runner
- Form a 'V' between your fingers and thumb to receive the baton
- Keep your receiving arm straight and still at above hip height and near shoulder height
- Grip the baton tightly and sprint away

### Incoming runner

- Pass the baton with a downward, forward-pushing motion into the outgoing runner's hand
- Place the upper third (furthest part) of the baton firmly into the hand of the outgoing runner

## ■ Health and safety

- Warm-up correctly before starting to sprint (see warm-ups section)
- The person behind (incoming runners) should run to the side of the person in front (outgoing runners) to avoid tripping him/her
- The outgoing runner should set off early enough to avoid the incoming runner running into him/her, or having to slow down suddenly
- Do not run across the path of others

## ■ Life skills

### Communication and interpersonal

- Communicate in a co-operative and friendly manner with others in your group
- Encourage each other to achieve the best group time you can
- Give each other positive and constructive feedback on your effort and technique

### Decision-making and critical thinking

- Set yourself realistic and achievable goals
- Keep re-evaluating and setting new goals

### Self-management

- Set up the challenge quickly and efficiently
- Challenge yourself to your maximum ability
- Don't give up or cheat if the challenge gets difficult
- Maximise your activity time and allow enough time to recover between attempts

# Relays 5

### Equipment

Relay baton

### Challenge

- In groups of 4–8 runners, work out the following for a 400m (1 lap) relay:
  - how far each person will run (min 50m, max 150m) (choose your distances)
  - which order you will run in
  - how you will exchange the baton
- Ignore the relay boxes and position yourselves around the track (choose where to stand)
- Perform a time trial over 400m (1 lap of a standard athletics track)
- Ask someone to time how long it takes you to complete the lap
- Record your time as a future target to improve upon
- Evaluate your performance and make any changes to try to improve your time

### Technique tips

**UPSWEEP BATON EXCHANGE**

**Outgoing runner**
- Present the palm of your receiving hand facing towards the incoming runner
- Form a 'V' between your fingers and thumb to receive the baton
- Keep your receiving arm straight and still at about hip height
- Grip the baton tightly and sprint away

**Incoming runner**
- Pass the baton with an upward-pushing motion into the outgoing runner's hand
- Place the nearest part of the baton firmly and as far as possible into the hand of the outgoing runner

© 2011 Kevin Morgan, *Athletics Challenges*, Routledge.

## DOWNSWEEP BATON EXCHANGE

### Outgoing runner
- Present the palm of your receiving hand facing upwards and towards the incoming runner
- Form a 'V' between your fingers and thumb to receive the baton
- Keep your receiving arm straight and still at above hip height and near shoulder height
- Grip the baton tightly and sprint away

### Incoming runner
- Pass the baton with a downward, forward-pushing motion into the outgoing runner's hand
- Place the upper third (furthest part) of the baton firmly into the hand of the outgoing runner

## ▬ Health and safety

- Warm-up correctly before starting to sprint (see warm-ups section)
- The person behind (incoming runners) should run to the side of the person in front (outgoing runners) to avoid tripping him/her
- The outgoing runner should set off early enough to avoid the incoming runner running into him/her, or having to slow down suddenly
- Do not run across the path of others

## ▬ Life skills

### Communication and interpersonal

- Communicate in a co-operative and friendly manner with others in your group
- Encourage each other to achieve the best group time you can
- Give each other positive and constructive feedback on your effort and technique

### Decision-making and critical thinking

- Choose the best distance between cones 3 and 4 to challenge yourself
- Set yourself realistic and achievable goals
- Keep re-evaluating and setting new goals

### Self-management

- Set up the challenge quickly and efficiently
- Challenge yourself to your maximum ability
- Don't give up or cheat if the challenge gets difficult
- Maximise your activity time and allow enough time to recover between attempts

© 2011 Kevin Morgan, *Athletics Challenges*, Routledge.

# Relays 6

## ■ Equipment

Relay baton, 4 cones, stopwatch, tape measure (optional)

## ■ Challenge

- Work in groups of 5
- Place a cone every 100m around a 400m running track
- Decide on your running order and position yourselves around the track with numbers 1 and 5 at the start and numbers 2, 3 and 4 by the other three cones
- Run a continuous relay for 2, 3 or 4 minutes (choose your time)
- Use your preferred method of exchanging the baton
- Ask someone to time you and work out the total distance covered in your chosen time, or do this yourselves
- Following a recovery, make further attempts to try to improve your overall group distance
- Record your best distance as a future target to improve upon

## ■ Technique tips

### UPSWEEP BATON EXCHANGE

**Outgoing runner**
- Present the palm of your receiving hand facing towards the incoming runner
- Form a 'V' between your fingers and thumb to receive the baton
- Keep your receiving arm straight and still at about hip height
- Grip the baton tightly and sprint away

**Incoming runner**
- Pass the baton with an upward-pushing motion into the outgoing runner's hand
- Place the nearest part of the baton firmly and as far as possible into the hand of the outgoing runner

## DOWNSWEEP BATON EXCHANGE

### Outgoing runner
- Present the palm of your receiving hand facing upwards and towards the incoming runner
- Form a 'V' between your fingers and thumb to receive the baton
- Keep your receiving arm straight and still at above hip height and near shoulder height
- Grip the baton tightly and sprint away

### Incoming runner
- Pass the baton with a downward, forward-pushing motion into the outgoing runner's hand
- Place the upper third (furthest part) of the baton firmly into the hand of the outgoing runner

## ■ Health and safety

- Warm-up correctly before starting to sprint (see warm-ups section)
- The person behind (incoming runners) should run to the side of the person in front (outgoing runners) to avoid tripping him/her
- The outgoing runner should set off early enough to avoid the incoming runner running into him/her, or having to slow down suddenly
- Do not run across the path of others

## ■ Life skills

### Communication and interpersonal

- Communicate in a co-operative and friendly manner with others in your group
- Encourage each other to achieve the best group distance that you can
- Give each other positive and constructive feedback on your effort and technique

### Decision-making and critical thinking

- Choose the best time to challenge yourselves
- Set yourself realistic and achievable goals
- Keep re-evaluating and setting new goals

### Self-management

- Set up the challenge quickly and efficiently
- Challenge yourself to your maximum ability
- Don't give up or cheat if the challenge gets difficult
- Maximise your activity time and allow enough time to recover between attempts

# Long jump 1

### ■ Equipment

2 cones, tape measure (optional)

### ■ Challenge

- Place one cone down as a starting mark
- Ask someone to mark with a cone where your heels land and perform the following jumps from a standing start:
    - two feet to two feet
    - one foot to the same foot
    - one to the other foot
    - one to two feet
- Make further attempts to try to beat your personal best distances
- Work out the best jump for distance from a standing start
- Measure your best distances with a tape measure or your own feet and record them as future targets to improve upon

### ■ Technique tips

- Drive powerfully off your take-off foot/feet
- Swing both arms vigorously forwards and upwards at take-off
- Pick up your knees in flight
- Land with your body weight forward, your hips low and your feet under your hips

## ■ Health and safety

- Warm-up correctly before starting to jump (see warm-ups section)
- Ensure that the jumping area is flat, dry and not slippery
- Practise your take-offs and landings at less than full effort before starting the challenge
- Land with your body weight forward and your hips low to the ground to avoid slipping
- If landing on a firm surface (not into a sandpit), land with your feet directly under your hips
- Ensure that you have plenty of space to jump into and that you are not jumping across the path of others

## ■ Life skills

### Communication and interpersonal

- Communicate in a co-operative and friendly manner with others
- Encourage others to challenge themselves and achieve the best distances they can
- Give others positive and constructive feedback on their effort and technique

### Decision-making and critical thinking

- Set yourself realistic and achievable goals
- Keep re-evaluating and setting new goals

### Self-management

- Set up the challenge quickly and efficiently
- Challenge yourself to your maximum ability
- Focus on improving your own personal best
- Don't give up or cheat if the challenge gets difficult
- Maximise your activity time, allowing enough time to recover between attempts

© 2011 Kevin Morgan, *Athletics Challenges*, Routledge.

# Long jump 2

### ▪▪▪ Equipment

2 cones, tape measure (optional)

### ▪▪▪ Challenge

- Place one cone down as a starting mark
- Ask someone to mark with a cone where your heels land and perform the following jumps from a 2–3-stride run-up:
  - two feet to two feet
  - one foot to the same foot
  - one to the other foot
  - one to two feet
- Make further attempts to try to beat your personal best distances
- Work out the best jump for distance from a 2–3-stride run-up
- Measure your best distances with a tape measure or your own feet and record them as future targets to improve upon

### ▪▪▪ Technique tips

- Drive powerfully off your take-off foot/feet
- Swing both arms vigorously forwards and upwards at take-off
- Pick up your knees in flight
- Land with your body weight forward, your hips low and your feet under your hips

## ■ Health and safety

- Warm-up correctly before starting to jump (see warm-ups section)
- Ensure that the jumping area is flat, dry and not slippery
- Don't take more than 2/3 strides
- Practise your take-offs and landings at less than full effort before starting the challenge
- Land with your body weight forward and your hips low to the ground to avoid slipping
- If landing on a firm surface (not into a sandpit), land with your feet directly under your hips
- Ensure that you have plenty of space to jump into and that you are not jumping across the path of others

## ■ Life skills

### Communication and interpersonal

- Communicate in a co-operative and friendly manner with others
- Encourage others to challenge themselves and achieve the best distances they can
- Give others positive and constructive feedback on their effort and technique

### Decision-making and critical thinking

- Set yourself realistic and achievable goals
- Keep re-evaluating and setting new goals

### Self-management

- Set up the challenge quickly and efficiently
- Challenge yourself to your maximum ability
- Focus on improving your own personal best
- Don't give up or cheat if the challenge gets difficult
- Maximise your activity time, allowing enough time to recover between attempts

# Long jump 3

### Equipment

2 cones, tape measure (optional)

### Challenge

- Place one cone down as a starting mark
- Perform 2, 3 or 4 consecutive two-footed jumps for distance (choose how many)
- Ask someone to mark the overall distance with a cone
- Following a recovery, make further attempts to beat your best distance
- Measure your best distances with a tape measure or your own feet and record them as future targets to improve upon

### Technique tips

- Place your feet about shoulder width apart
- Hold both arms behind your body to start
- Lean forwards until you are off balance
- Drive powerfully off both feet
- Swing both arms vigorously forwards and get them back quickly behind your body in time for the next jump
- Pick up your knees in flight
- Land with your body weight forward, your hips low and your feet under your hips

© 2011 Kevin Morgan, *Athletics Challenges*, Routledge.

## ■ Health and safety

- Warm-up correctly before starting to jump (see warm-ups section)
- Ensure that the jumping area is flat, dry and not slippery
- Practise your take-offs and landings at less than full effort before starting the challenge
- Land with your body weight forward and your hips low to the ground to avoid slipping
- Land with your feet directly under your hips for each jump
- Ensure that you have plenty of space to jump into and that you are not jumping across the path of others

## ■ Life skills

### Communication and interpersonal

- Communicate in a co-operative and friendly manner with others
- Encourage others to challenge themselves and achieve the best distance they can
- Give others positive and constructive feedback on their effort and technique

### Decision-making and critical thinking

- Choose the best number of jumps to challenge yourself
- Set yourself realistic and achievable goals
- Keep re-evaluating and setting new goals

### Self-management

- Set up the challenge quickly and efficiently
- Challenge yourself to your maximum ability
- Focus on improving your own personal best
- Don't give up or cheat if the challenge gets difficult
- Maximise your activity time, allowing enough time to recover between attempts

# Long jump 4

### ■■■ Equipment

2 cones, tape measure (optional)

### ■■■ Challenge

- Place 2 cones 10, 15 or 20m apart (choose your distance)
- Perform the lowest possible number of 'bounds' (big strides fully extending the back leg) on each leg to cover the distance
- Try to reduce the number of 'bounds'
- Record your lowest number of 'bounds' for each leg and the distance covered as a future target to improve upon

### ■■■ Technique tips

- Start on one foot with both arms behind your body
- Lean forwards until you are slightly off balance
- Drive powerfully off one foot for each 'bound'
- Swing your arms vigorously and get them back quickly into position in time for the next 'bound'
- Pick up your leading knee in flight
- Land flat-footed and immediately spring into the next 'bound'

Section 2

### ■ Health and safety

- Warm-up correctly before starting to jump (see warm-ups section)
- Ensure that the jumping area is flat, dry and not slippery
- Practise 'bounding' at less than full effort before starting the challenge
- Ensure that you have plenty of space and that you are not jumping across the path of others

### ■ Life skills

**Communication and interpersonal**

- Communicate in a co-operative and friendly manner with others
- Encourage others to challenge themselves and achieve the best performance they can
- Give others positive and constructive feedback on their effort and technique

**Decision-making and critical thinking**

- Choose the best distance to challenge yourself
- Set yourself realistic and achievable goals
- Keep re-evaluating and setting new goals

**Self-management**

- Set up the challenge quickly and efficiently
- Challenge yourself to your maximum ability
- Focus on improving your own personal best
- Don't give up or cheat if the challenge gets difficult
- Maximise your activity time, allowing enough time to recover between attempts

# Long jump 5

### ▇ Equipment

2 cones, tape measure (optional)

### ▇ Challenge

- Place one cone down as a starting mark
- From a standing start, sprint for 9, 11 or 13 strides (choose how many)
- Ask someone to mark with a cone where your last stride lands
- Following a recovery, make further attempts whilst trying to place your take-off foot in line with the marked cone each time
- Measure the distance with a tape measure or with your own feet and record it to use in the long jump

### ▇ Technique tips

- Start with your non-take-off foot forwards
- Step onto your take-off foot with your first stride
- Run fast, but at a pace at which you could take-off
- Drive off the ground with each stride and pick up your knees in front of your body
- Drive your arms forwards and backwards
- Run fast, but relaxed
- Try not to look down at the cone

© 2011 Kevin Morgan, *Athletics Challenges*, Routledge.

## ■ Health and safety

- Warm-up correctly before starting to run (see warm-ups section)
- Ensure that the running area is flat, dry and not slippery
- Do not cross the path of other runners

## ■ Life skills

### Communication and interpersonal

- Communicate in a co-operative and friendly manner with others
- Encourage others to challenge themselves and achieve accuracy in their run-up
- Give others positive and constructive feedback on their effort and technique

### Decision-making and critical thinking

- Choose the best number of strides to maximise your speed at take-off
- Re-evaluate and set new goals if necessary

### Self-management

- Set up the challenge quickly and efficiently
- Challenge yourself to your maximum ability
- Don't give up or cheat if the challenge gets difficult
- Maximise your activity time, allowing enough time to recover between attempts

# Long jump 6

### ■ Equipment

Sandpit, tape measure, rake, brush

### ■ Challenge

- Work out your run-up using 9, 11 or 13 sprinting strides (choose how many) and mark your starting point with a cone
- Perform a run-up and long jump into a sandpit
- Ask someone to measure the jump using a tape measure
- Following a recovery, make further attempts to try to beat your personal best distance
- Measure and record your best distance as a future target to improve upon

### ■ Technique tips

**Approach**
- Start the approach by stepping onto your take-off foot
- Use checkmarks to develop an accurate approach
- Use good sprinting form showing high knee lift and good leg drive
- Run fast, but at a pace at which you can take-off effectively
- Stay relaxed – don't strain for extra speed at the board

**Take-off**
- Your posture should be upright
- Place your take-off foot well ahead of your hips
- Concentrate on running off the board and achieving height
- Drive your non-take-off leg and both arms upwards

**Flight**
- Extend your leading leg so that you assume a stride position in the air
- Look forward towards the end of the pit

**Landing**
- Push both legs forwards for landing
- Push your feet out ahead of your body
- Reach forwards with your arms in flight and then backwards on landing
- Try not to fall backwards after landing

© 2011 Kevin Morgan, *Athletics Challenges*, Routledge.

## ■ Health and safety

- Warm-up correctly before starting to jump (see warm-ups section)
- Ensure that the running area is flat, dry and not slippery
- Ensure that the sandpit is safe, raked and free of debris
- Do not cross the path of others

## ■ Life skills

### Communication and interpersonal

- Communicate in a co-operative and friendly manner with others
- Encourage others to challenge themselves and achieve the best distance they can
- Give others positive and constructive feedback on their effort and technique

### Decision-making and critical thinking

- Choose the best number of strides to maximise your speed at take-off
- Set yourself realistic and achievable goals
- Keep re-evaluating and setting new goals

### Self-management

- Set up the challenge quickly and efficiently
- Challenge yourself to your maximum ability
- Focus on improving your own personal best
- Don't give up or cheat if the challenge gets difficult
- Maximise your activity time, allowing enough time to recover between attempts

# Triple jump 1

## ■■■ Equipment

2 cones, tape measure (optional)

## ■■■ Challenge

- Place one cone down as a starting mark
- Ask someone to mark with a cone where your heels land and perform the following jumps from a standing start:
    - 2 or 3 hops (choose how many)
    - 2 or 3 strides (choose how many)
    - hop-hop-stride
    - stride-stride-hop
    - stride-hop-stride
    - hop-stride-hop
    - hop-stride-jump
- Make further attempts to try to beat your personal best distances
- Work out the best multiple jump for distance from a standing start
- Measure your best distances with a tape measure or your own feet and record them as future targets to improve upon

## ■■■ Technique tips

- Drive powerfully off your take-off foot for each phase
- Swing your arms vigorously for each phase
- Pick up your leading knee in flight
- Look straight ahead
- Keep your body upright
- At the end of the final phase, land with your body weight forward, your hips low and your foot/feet under your hips

© 2011 Kevin Morgan, *Athletics Challenges*, Routledge.

## ■ Health and safety

- Warm-up correctly before starting to jump (see warm-ups section)
- Ensure that the jumping area is flat, dry and not slippery
- Practise your take-offs and landings at less than full effort before starting the challenge
- Land with your body weight forward and your hips low to the ground to avoid slipping
- If landing on a firm surface (not into a sandpit), land with your foot/feet directly under your hips
- Ensure that you have plenty of space to jump into and that you are not jumping across the path of others

## ■ Life skills

### Communication and interpersonal

- Communicate in a co-operative and friendly manner with others
- Encourage others to challenge themselves and achieve the best distances they can
- Give others positive and constructive feedback on their effort and technique

### Decision-making and critical thinking

- Choose the best number of jumps to challenge yourself
- Set yourself realistic and achievable goals
- Keep re-evaluating and setting new goals

### Self-management

- Set up the challenge quickly and efficiently
- Challenge yourself to your maximum ability
- Focus on improving your own personal best
- Don't give up or cheat if the challenge gets difficult
- Maximise your activity time, allowing enough time to recover between attempts

# Triple jump 2

### ■ Equipment

2 cones, tape measure (optional)

### ■ Challenge

- Place one cone down as a starting mark
- Ask someone to mark with a cone where your heels land and perform the following jumps from a 2–3-stride run-up:
    - 2 or 3 hops (choose how many)
    - 2 or 3 strides (choose how many)
    - hop-hop-stride
    - stride-stride-hop
    - stride-hop-stride
    - hop-stride-hop
    - hop-stride-jump
- Make further attempts to try to beat your personal best distances
- Work out the best multiple jump for distance from a standing start
- Measure your best distances with a tape measure or your own foot/feet and record them as future targets to improve upon

### ■ Technique tips

- Drive powerfully off your take-off foot for each phase
- Swing your arms vigorously for each phase
- Pick up your leading knee in flight
- Look straight ahead
- Keep your body upright
- At the end of the final phase, land with your body weight forward, your hips low and your foot under your hips

## Health and safety

- Warm-up correctly before starting to jump (see warm-ups section)
- Ensure that the jumping area is flat, dry and not slippery
- Don't take more than 2/3 strides
- Practise your take-offs and landings at less than full effort before starting the challenge
- Land with your body weight forward and your hips low to the ground to avoid slipping
- If landing on a firm surface (not into a sandpit), land with your foot/feet directly under your hips
- Ensure that you have plenty of space to jump into and that you are not jumping across the path of others

## Life skills

### Communication and interpersonal

- Communicate in a co-operative and friendly manner with others
- Encourage others to challenge themselves and achieve the best distances they can
- Give others positive and constructive feedback on their effort and technique

### Decision-making and critical thinking

- Choose the best number of jumps to challenge yourself
- Set yourself realistic and achievable goals
- Keep re-evaluating and setting new goals

### Self-management

- Set up the challenge quickly and efficiently
- Challenge yourself to your maximum ability
- Focus on improving your own personal best
- Don't give up if the challenge gets difficult
- Maximise your activity time, allowing enough time to recover between attempts

© 2011 Kevin Morgan, *Athletics Challenges*, Routledge.

# Triple jump 3

### ■ Equipment

2 cones, tape measure (optional)

### ■ Challenge

- Place 2 cones 10, 12 or 15m apart (choose your distance)
- Perform the lowest possible number of hops on each leg to cover the distance
- Try to reduce the number of hops
- Record your lowest number of hops for each leg and the distance covered as a future target to improve upon

### ■ Technique tips

- Start on one foot with both arms behind your body
- Lean forwards until you are slightly off balance
- Drive powerfully off one foot
- Swing your arms vigorously and get them back quickly into position in time for the next hop
- Pick up your leading knee in flight
- Land flat-footed and immediately spring into the next hop

© 2011 Kevin Morgan, *Athletics Challenges*, Routledge.

## ■ Health and safety

- Warm-up correctly before starting to jump (see warm-ups section)
- Ensure that the jumping area is flat, dry and not slippery
- Practise hopping at less than full effort before starting the challenge
- Ensure that you have plenty of space and that you are not jumping across the path of others

## ■ Life skills

### Communication and interpersonal

- Communicate in a co-operative and friendly manner with others
- Encourage others to challenge themselves and achieve the best performance they can
- Give others positive and constructive feedback on their effort and technique

### Decision-making and critical thinking

- Choose the best distance to challenge yourself
- Set yourself realistic and achievable goals
- Keep re-evaluating and setting new goals

### Self-management

- Set up the challenge quickly and efficiently
- Challenge yourself to your maximum ability
- Focus on improving your own personal best
- Don't give up or cheat if the challenge gets difficult
- Maximise your activity time, allowing enough time to recover between attempts

# Triple jump 4

### ■ Equipment

4 cones/hoops, tape measure (optional)

### ■ Challenge

- Place 1 cone as a starting mark and 3 other cones/hoops about a metre apart (choose your distance)
- From a standing start, perform a hop, stride ('bound') and jump, trying to land beside a cone, or in a hoop, on each phase
- Increase the distances equally between the cones/hoops to challenge yourself
- Measure the distance between each cone/hoop and the total distance with a tape measure or your own feet as a future target to improve upon
- Following a recovery, repeat the process using a 2–3-stride run-up

### ■ Technique tips

- Take-off on your preferred hopping foot
- For the first phase, hop powerfully off one foot and land on the same foot
- Immediately take a big stride ('bound') from one foot to the other, for the second phase
- Finally, jump from one foot to two feet to land
- Swing your arms vigorously and get them back quickly into position in time for the next phase
- Look straight ahead
- Land in the final phase with your body weight forwards and your hips low

## Health and safety

- Warm-up correctly before starting to jump (see warm-ups section)
- Ensure that the jumping area is flat, dry and not slippery
- Practise jumping at less than full effort before starting the challenge
- Ensure that you have plenty of space and that you are not jumping across the path of others

## Life skills

### Communication and interpersonal

- Communicate in a co-operative and friendly manner with others
- Encourage others to challenge themselves and achieve the best distances they can
- Give others positive and constructive feedback on their effort and technique

### Decision-making and critical thinking

- Choose the best distance between cones to challenge yourself
- Set yourself realistic and achievable goals
- Keep re-evaluating and setting new goals

### Self-management

- Set up the challenge quickly and efficiently
- Challenge yourself to your maximum ability
- Focus on improving your own personal best
- Don't give up or cheat if the challenge gets difficult
- Maximise your activity time, allowing enough time to recover between attempts

# Triple jump 5

### ▪▪▪ Equipment

2 cones, tape measure (optional)

### ▪▪▪ Challenge

- Place one cone down as a starting mark
- From standing, sprint for 7, 9 or 11 strides (choose how many)
- Ask someone to mark with a cone where your last stride lands
- Following a recovery, make further attempts whilst trying to place your take-off foot in line with the marked cone each time
- Measure the distance with a tape measure or with your own feet and record it to use in the long jump

### ▪▪▪ Technique tips

- Start with your non-take-off foot forwards
- Step on to your take-off foot with your first stride
- Run fast, but at a pace at which you could take-off for the hop phase
- Drive off the ground with each stride and pick up your knees in front of your body
- Drive your arms forwards and backwards
- Run fast, but relaxed
- Try not to look down at the cone

## ■ Health and safety

- Warm-up correctly before starting to run (see warm-ups section)
- Ensure that the running area is flat, dry and not slippery
- Do not cross the path of other runners

## ■ Life skills

### Communication and interpersonal

- Communicate in a co-operative and friendly manner with others
- Encourage others to challenge themselves and achieve accuracy in their run-up
- Give others positive and constructive feedback on their effort and technique

### Decision-making and critical thinking

- Choose the best number of strides to maximise your speed at take-off
- Re-evaluate and set new goals if necessary

### Self-management

- Set up the challenge quickly and efficiently
- Challenge yourself to your maximum ability
- Don't give up or cheat if the challenge gets difficult
- Maximise your activity time, allowing enough time to recover between attempts

# Triple jump 6

## ■ Equipment

Sandpit, cones, tape measure, rake, brush

## ■ Challenge

- Work out your run-up using 7, 9 or 11 sprinting strides (choose how many) and mark your starting point with a cone
- Perform a run-up and triple jump into a sandpit
- Ask someone to measure the jump using a tape measure
- Following a recovery, make further attempts to try to beat your personal best distance
- Measure and record your best distance as a future target to improve upon

## ■ Technique tips

### Approach
- Start the approach by stepping onto your take-off foot
- Use checkmarks to develop consistency
- Use good sprinting form, showing high knee lift and good leg drive
- Run fast but at a speed from which you can take-off in the hop and step phases effectively

### Hop
- Use a fairly low take-off angle for the hop phase
- Pull the heel of your take-off leg back under your seat and then push it forward for the landing
- Keep your body upright and look forwards towards the end of the pit

### Stride/bound
- Push hard off your take-off leg
- Use quite a low take-off angle
- Pick up the thigh of your non-take-off leg
- Maintain an upright body position

### Jump
- Go for height at take-off
- Keep your head and chest up
- Look forwards towards the end of the pit

© 2011 Kevin Morgan, *Athletics Challenges*, Routledge.

**Final landing**
- Push both legs forwards for landing
- Push your feet out ahead of your body
- Reach forwards with your arms in flight and then backwards on landing
- Try not to fall backwards after landing

## Health and safety

- Warm-up correctly before starting to jump (see warm-ups section)
- Ensure that the running area is flat, dry and not slippery
- Ensure that the sandpit is safe, raked and free of debris
- Choose your take-off board or mark your own with cones, so that you are comfortably reaching the sandpit in your final jump phase
- Do not cross the path of others

## Life skills

### Communication and interpersonal

- Communicate in a co-operative and friendly manner with others
- Encourage others to challenge themselves and achieve the best distance they can
- Give others positive and constructive feedback on their effort and technique

### Decision-making and critical thinking

- Choose the best number of strides to maximise your speed at take-off
- Set yourself realistic and achievable goals
- Keep re-evaluating and setting new goals

### Self-management

- Set up the challenge quickly and efficiently
- Challenge yourself to your maximum ability
- Focus on improving your own personal best
- Don't give up or cheat if the challenge gets difficult
- Maximise your activity time, allowing enough time to recover between attempts

# High jump 1

### ■■■ Equipment

Vertical jump board, or chalk and metre ruler

### ■■■ Challenge

- Use a vertical jump board or, alternatively, hold a piece of chalk, and standing facing the wall, feet together and toes touching the wall, reach up as high as you can with both hands and make a chalk mark on the wall
- Turn to stand sideways on to the vertical jump board/wall
- Bend your knees and jump as high as you can
- Mark the board/wall with the chalk at the highest point of your jump
- Measure the distance between the standing and jumping marks and record it as a future target to improve upon

### ■■■ Technique tips

- Place your feet shoulder-width apart
- Start with your arms by your sides
- Drive powerfully off both feet
- Swing both arms vigorously upwards
- Reach up as high as you can with one hand to make the mark

## ■ Health and safety

- Warm-up correctly before starting to jump (see warm-ups section)
- Jump straight up and not in towards the wall
- Bend your knees on landing

## ■ Life skills

### Communication and interpersonal

- Communicate in a co-operative and friendly manner with others
- Encourage others to challenge themselves and achieve the best height they can
- Give others positive and constructive feedback on their effort and technique

### Decision-making and critical thinking

- Set yourself realistic and achievable goals
- Keep re-evaluating and setting new goals

### Self-management

- Set up the challenge quickly and efficiently
- Challenge yourself to your maximum ability
- Focus on improving your own personal best
- Don't give up or cheat if the challenge gets difficult
- Maximise your activity time, allowing enough time to recover between attempts

# High jump 2

### Equipment

4–6 two-way foam wedge/plastic hurdles, 1 stopwatch

### Challenge

- Work in groups of 4–6
- Place 4–6 (choose the number and height) two-way foam wedge/plastic hurdles in a line with a short space (approximately 1m) between each, as shown below

―――  ―――  ―――  ―――  ―――  ―――

- Take it in turns to move along the line of hurdles doing a one-foot-to-the-other scissors jump over each one
- Work for a set time (e.g. 2 minutes) or time how long it takes for each group member to move to the end of the line of hurdles in turn
- Following a recovery, make further attempts to try to improve your team time or total
- Record your best time or number of repetitions the team complete in the set time as a future target to improve upon

### Technique tips

- Jump from left to right and then right to left, or vice versa, along the line of hurdles
- Swing your arms upwards when jumping
- Swing your inside leg upwards and parallel to the ground
- Keep your upper body straight and upright
- Look straight ahead
- Land on your feet

## ■ Health and safety

- Warm-up correctly before starting to jump (see warm-ups section)
- Jump upwards and try not to lean in towards the hurdles
- Land on your feet and bend your knees on landing

## ■ Life skills

### Communication and interpersonal

- Communicate in a co-operative and friendly manner with others
- Encourage others to challenge themselves and achieve the best time they can
- Give others positive and constructive feedback on their effort and technique

### Decision-making and critical thinking

- Set yourself realistic and achievable goals
- Keep re-evaluating and setting new goals

### Self-management

- Set up the challenge quickly and efficiently
- Challenge yourself to your maximum ability
- Focus on improving your own personal best
- Don't give up or cheat if the challenge gets difficult
- Maximise your activity time, allowing enough time to recover between attempts

# High jump 3

### ■■■ Equipment

Bamboo cane/stick, tape measure (optional)

### ■■■ Challenge

- Work in pairs and ask your partner to hold a bamboo cane or stick at a height you can comfortably scissors-jump over (choose your height)
- Stand alongside your partner on the same side as your preferred take-off foot
- Perform a scissors jump over the bamboo cane/stick, jumping away from your partner
- Ask your partner to adjust the height until you reach your limit
- Measure the jump in relation to your height (e.g. waist height), or use a tape measure and record it as a future target to improve upon
- Change with your partner

### ■■■ Technique tips

- Jump from left to right or right to left, as you prefer
- Take a 2–3-stride run-up
- Swing your arms upwards when jumping
- Swing your inside leg upwards and parallel to the ground
- Keep your upper body straight and upright
- Look straight ahead
- Land on your feet

## Health and safety

- Warm-up correctly before starting to jump (see warm-ups section)
- Be careful when handling the bamboo canes/sticks
- Keep the bamboo cane/stick completely still and parallel to the ground when your partner is jumping
- Jump away from your partner to avoid any chance of kicking him/her
- Don't take-off too close to the bamboo cane/stick
- Jump straight up and try not to lean in towards the bamboo cane/stick
- Bend your knees on landing

## Life skills

### Communication and interpersonal

- Communicate in a co-operative and friendly manner with others
- Encourage others to challenge themselves and achieve the best height they can
- Give others positive and constructive feedback on their effort and technique

### Decision-making and critical thinking

- Choose the best height to challenge yourself
- Set yourself realistic and achievable goals
- Keep re-evaluating and setting new goals

### Self-management

- Set up the challenge quickly and efficiently
- Challenge yourself to your maximum ability
- Focus on improving your own personal best
- Don't give up or cheat if the challenge gets difficult
- Maximise your activity time, allowing enough time to recover between attempts

# High jump 4

### ■ Equipment

High-jump posts and landing mats, high-jump bar, cones

### ■ Challenge

- Using cones, mark a 3–5 stride (choose the number of strides) run-up at an angle of about 35–40 degrees to the bar

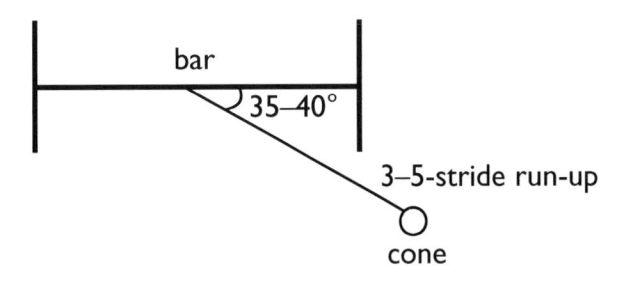

- Set the bar at your chosen height
- Run up and perform a high jump using the scissors technique
- Adjust the height until you reach your limit
- Record your best height as a future target to improve upon

### ■ Technique tips

- Jump from the right or left side, as you prefer
- Take a 3–5-stride run-up at an angle of about 35–40 degrees to the bar
- Swing your arms upwards when jumping
- Swing your inside leg upwards and parallel to the ground to clear the bar
- Keep your upper body straight and upright
- Look straight ahead
- Land on your feet

## ■ Health and safety

- Warm-up correctly before starting to jump (see warm-ups section)
- Use landing mats to absorb your body weight on landing
- Land on your feet
- Bend your knees on landing

## ■ Life skills

### Communication and interpersonal

- Communicate in a co-operative and friendly manner with others
- Encourage others to challenge themselves and achieve the best height they can
- Give others positive and constructive feedback on their effort and technique

### Decision-making and critical thinking

- Choose the best height to challenge yourself
- Set yourself realistic and achievable goals
- Keep re-evaluating and setting new goals

### Self-management

- Set up the challenge quickly and efficiently
- Challenge yourself to your maximum ability
- Focus on improving your own personal best
- Don't give up or cheat if the challenge gets difficult
- Maximise your activity time, allowing enough time to recover between attempts

# High jump 5

### ■■■ Equipment

Foam/soft ball, ball net, basketball hoop/held pole, cones

### ■■■ Challenge

- Place a foam/soft ball in a ball net and tie it to a basketball hoop or held pole
- Using cones, mark a 5–7 stride (choose the number of strides), J-shaped run-up to take-off under the ball

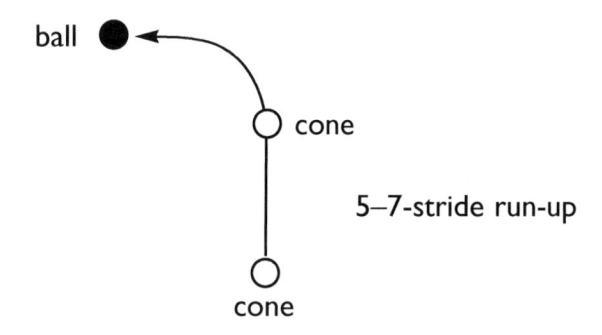

```
ball  ●◀──┐
          │
        ○ cone
        │
        │   5–7-stride run-up
        │
        ○
       cone
```

- Run up and jump, taking off from the outside foot, to head the ball or, alternatively, try to touch the ball with your inside arm instead of heading it
- Adjust the height of the ball to challenge yourself to reach your limit

### ■■■ Technique tips

- If using a held pole, ask the person holding it to stand on a platform so that the ball is high enough to make you jump high
- Make a fast and controlled J-shaped approach, with an upright body position
- At take-off, place your take-off foot slightly ahead of your body
- Your take-off leg should be slightly flexed at the knee
- Try not to lean towards the ball before take-off
- Drive directly upwards off your jumping foot

## Section 2

### ■ Health and safety

- Warm-up correctly before starting to jump (see warm-ups section)
- If using a held pole, point it upwards and hold it high enough so that there is no chance of the jumper colliding with it
- Jump straight up and try not to lean in towards the ball
- Bend your knees on landing

### ■ Life skills

#### Communication and interpersonal

- Communicate in a co-operative and friendly manner with others
- Encourage others to challenge themselves and achieve the best height they can
- Give others positive and constructive feedback on their effort and technique

#### Decision-making and critical thinking

- Set yourself realistic and achievable goals
- Keep re-evaluating and setting new goals

#### Self-management

- Set up the challenge quickly and efficiently
- Challenge yourself to your maximum ability
- Focus on improving your own personal best
- Don't give up or cheat if the challenge gets difficult
- Maximise your activity time, allowing enough time to recover between attempts

# High jump 6

### ■■■ Equipment

High-jump bed and posts, bar/elastic bar, cones

### ■■■ Challenge

- Using cones, mark a 5–7 stride (choose the number of strides) J-shaped run-up

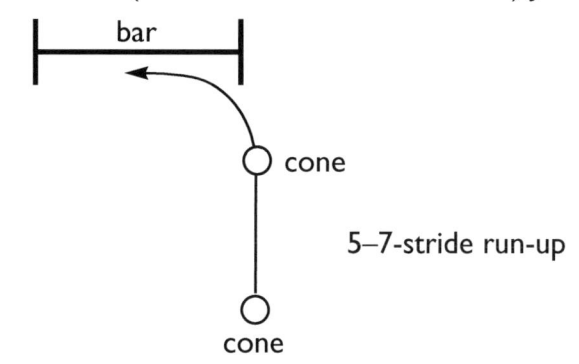

```
|———— bar ————|
        ←
        ○ cone
              5–7-stride run-up
        ○
        cone
```

- Set the bar at your chosen height
- Run up and perform a high jump using the Fosbury flop technique
- Adjust the height until you reach your limit
- Record your best height as a future target to improve upon

### ■■■ Technique tips

- Make a fast and controlled J-shaped approach, with an upright body position
- Take off about an arm's distance away from the bar and about a quarter of the crossbar's length in from the nearest upright
- On take-off, place your take-off foot slightly ahead of your body
- Your take-off leg should be slightly flexed before take-off
- Try not to lean towards the bar before take-off
- Drive directly upwards off your jumping foot
- Use your arms to assist take-off
- Turn your body in flight so that you are jumping backwards over the bar
- When your shoulders cross the bar, your hips should be pushed upwards
- Both legs should be bent at the knee as you clear the bar
- Once your seat has crossed the bar, your legs should straighten
- Land on your back and shoulders

## ■ Health and safety

- Warm-up correctly before starting to jump (see warm-ups section)
- Do not attempt the Fosbury flop without the use of a **full high-jump bed**
- Ensure that you have been taught the basic progressions for Fosbury flop before attempting this challenge
- Land on your upper back and shoulders

## ■ Life skills

### Communication and interpersonal

- Communicate in a co-operative and friendly manner with others
- Encourage others to challenge themselves and achieve the best height they can
- Give others positive and constructive feedback on their effort and technique

### Decision-making and critical thinking

- Choose the best height to challenge yourself
- Set yourself realistic and achievable goals
- Keep re-evaluating and setting new goals

### Self-management

- Set up the challenge quickly and efficiently
- Challenge yourself to your maximum ability
- Focus on improving your own personal best
- Don't give up or cheat if the challenge gets difficult
- Maximise your activity time, allowing enough time to recover between attempts

# Shot put 1

### ■■■ Equipment

Weighted ball or soccer/basketball, 4 cones, tape measure

### ■■■ Challenge

- Place 2 cones as a throwing line
- Sit behind the line facing the direction of the throw with your legs out straight in front of you or in straddle-sit position
- Using a weighted ball (choose your weight) or soccer/basketball, perform a sitting put (push throw) for distance
- Ask someone to mark the distance with a cone
- Make further attempts to try to beat your personal best distance
- Measure and record your best distance as a future target to improve upon
- Repeat the process from a kneeling position facing the direction of the put

### ■■■ Technique tips

- Hold the ball on your preferred shoulder or on your chest, using one or two hands
- Push your chest upward to begin the put
- Your arm/arms should be 'last and fast'
- Extend your fingers to complete the put
- Focus on the principles of 'low to high' and 'slow to fast'

© 2011 Kevin Morgan, *Athletics Challenges*, Routledge.

## ▰ Health and safety

- Warm-up correctly before starting to throw (see warm-ups section)
- Ensure that you communicate with the person marking your throw and that he/she is in a safe position before you start
- Ensure that you have plenty of space either side of you when throwing
- Carry or roll the ball back safely to the throwing line between attempts

## ▰ Life skills

### Communication and interpersonal

- Communicate in a co-operative and friendly manner with others
- Encourage others to challenge themselves and achieve the best distance they can
- Give others positive and constructive feedback on their effort and technique

### Decision-making and critical thinking

- Choose the best weight ball to challenge yourself
- Set yourself realistic and achievable goals
- Keep re-evaluating and setting new goals

### Self-management

- Set up the challenge quickly and efficiently
- Challenge yourself to your maximum ability
- Focus on improving your own personal best
- Don't give up or cheat if the challenge gets difficult
- Maximise your activity time, allowing enough time to recover between attempts

# Shot put 2

### ■ Equipment

Weighted ball or soccer/basketball, 4 cones, tape measure

### ■ Challenge

- Place 2 cones as a throwing line
- Stand behind the line facing side on to the direction of the throw
- Using a weighted ball (choose your weight) or soccer/basketball, perform a standing put (push throw) for distance
- Ask someone to mark the distance with a cone
- Make further attempts to try to beat your personal best distance
- Measure and record your best distance as a future target to improve upon
- Repeat the process adding a side shift movement to the start of the put

### ■ Technique tips *(for right-handed throwers)*

- Hold the ball on your shoulder, using one or two hands
- Position your feet so that your left toe and your right heel are in line
- Bend your knees and extend them powerfully to begin the put
- Drive your right hip towards the direction of the put
- Push your chest forward and lift your body upwards
- Follow your chest with your shoulder
- Extend your fingers to complete the put
- For the side-shift movement, remain sideways on throughout and keep your upper body low
- Focus on the principles of 'low to high', 'slow to fast', 'legs first arm last' and transfer of weight from 'back to front'

## Health and safety

- Warm-up correctly before starting to throw (see warm-ups section)
- Ensure that you communicate with the person marking your throw and that he/she is in a safe position before you start
- Ensure that you have plenty of space either side of you when throwing
- Carry or roll the ball back safely to the throwing line between attempts

## Life skills

### Communication and interpersonal

- Communicate in a co-operative and friendly manner with others
- Encourage others to challenge themselves and achieve the best distance they can
- Give others positive and constructive feedback on their effort and technique

### Decision-making and critical thinking

- Choose the best weight ball to challenge yourself
- Set yourself realistic and achievable goals
- Keep re-evaluating and setting new goals

### Self-management

- Set up the challenge quickly and efficiently
- Challenge yourself to your maximum ability
- Focus on improving your own personal best
- Don't give up or cheat if the challenge gets difficult
- Maximise your activity time, allowing enough time to recover between attempts

# Shot put 3

### ■ Equipment

Weighted ball or soccer/basketball, 3 cones, tape measure

### ■ Challenge

- Place 2 cones as a throwing line
- Stand behind the line facing away from the direction of the throw
- Hold a weighted ball (choose your weight) or soccer/basketball in two hands between your legs and throw it backwards over your head for distance
- Ask someone to mark the distance with a cone
- Make further attempts to try to beat your personal best distance
- Measure and record your best distance as a future targets to improve upon

### ■ Technique tips

- Stand with your legs apart and hold the ball in two hands between your legs
- Swing the ball through your legs and then above and over your head
- Bend your knees and extend them powerfully to assist the throw
- Keep your back flat and your head up
- Keep your arms straight throughout the throw
- Release the ball above your head

## ■ Health and safety

- Warm-up correctly before starting to throw (see warm-ups section)
- Ensure that you communicate with the person marking your throw and that he/she is in a safe position before you start to throw
- Ensure that you have plenty of space either side of you when throwing
- Carry or roll the ball back safely to the throwing line between attempts

## ■ Life skills

### Communication and interpersonal

- Communicate in a co-operative and friendly manner with others
- Encourage others to challenge themselves and achieve the best distance they can
- Give others positive and constructive feedback on their effort and technique

### Decision-making and critical thinking

- Choose the best weight ball to challenge yourself
- Set yourself realistic and achievable goals
- Keep re-evaluating and setting new goals

### Self-management

- Set up the challenge quickly and efficiently
- Challenge yourself to your maximum ability
- Focus on improving your own personal best
- Don't give up or cheat if the challenge gets difficult
- Maximise your activity time, allowing enough time to recover between attempts

# Shot put 4

### ■ Equipment

Weighted ball or soccer/basketball, 2 cones, 4 plastic hoops

### ■ Challenge

- Work in groups of 4–5
- Place 2 cones as a throwing line and 4 hoops as targets (choose your distances and positions)
- Stand behind the line facing side on to the direction of the throw
- Using a weighted ball (choose your weight) or soccer/basketball, perform a series of standing puts (push throws) for accuracy, using the hoops as targets
- Devise a scoring system and decide on the number of throws allowed
- Make further attempts to try to beat your best score
- Record the scoring system, number of throws and your individual or team score as a future target to improve upon

### ■ Technique tips *(for right-handed throwers)*

- Hold the ball on your shoulder, using one or two hands
- Position your feet so that your left toe and right heel are in line
- Bend your knees and extend them powerfully to begin the put
- Drive your right hip towards the direction of the put
- Push your chest forward and lift your body upwards
- Follow your chest with your shoulder
- Extend your fingers to complete the put
- Focus on the principles of 'low to high', 'slow to fast', 'legs first arm last' and transfer of weight from 'back to front'

## Health and safety

- Warm-up correctly before starting to throw (see warm-ups section)
- Ensure everyone is in a safe position before you start to throw
- Ensure that you have plenty of space either side of you when throwing
- Carry or roll the ball back safely to the throwing line between attempts

## Life skills

### Communication and interpersonal

- Communicate in a co-operative and friendly manner with others
- Encourage others to challenge themselves and achieve the best score they can
- Give others positive and constructive feedback on their effort and technique

### Decision-making and critical thinking

- Choose the best weight ball, position of the hoops and number of attempts to challenge yourself
- Set yourself realistic and achievable goals
- Keep re-evaluating and setting new goals

### Self-management

- Set up the challenge quickly and efficiently
- Challenge yourself to your maximum ability
- Focus on improving your own personal best
- Don't give up or cheat if the challenge gets difficult
- Maximise your activity time, allowing enough time to recover between attempts

# Shot put 5

### ■■■ Equipment

Weighted ball or soccer/basketball, 4 cones, 4 plastic hoops

### ■■■ Challenge

- Work in groups of 4–5
- Place 4 cones as a throwing area (approx 2m x 2m) and 4 hoops as targets (choose your distances and positions)
- Stand at the back of the throwing area, facing away from the direction of the throw
- Using a weighted ball (choose your weight) or soccer/basketball, perform a series of rotational puts (push throws) for accuracy, using the hoops as targets
- Devise a scoring system and decide on the number of throws allowed
- Make further attempts to try to beat your best score
- Record the scoring system, number of throws and your individual or team score as a future target to improve upon

### ■■■ Technique tips *(for right-handed throwers)*

- Hold the ball tight and close to your neck throughout the throw
- Your legs should be slightly flexed and your vision to the rear of the circle
- Rotate your body by pivoting on the balls of your feet towards the direction of the put
- Continue to pivot on your left foot, whilst picking up your right foot and placing it in the middle of the throwing area
- Pick up your left foot and push it towards the front of the throwing area
- Extend upwards, driving your hips and chest toward the direction of the put
- Extend your arm and fingers to complete the put

© 2011 Kevin Morgan, *Athletics Challenges*, Routledge.

## ■ Health and safety

- Warm-up correctly before starting to throw (see warm-ups section)
- Ensure everyone is in a safe position before you start to throw
- Rotational throws can be difficult to control so allow extra space either side of you
- Carry or roll the ball back safely to the throwing line between attempts

## ■ Life skills

### Communication and interpersonal

- Communicate in a co-operative and friendly manner with others
- Encourage others to challenge themselves and achieve the best score they can
- Give others positive and constructive feedback on their effort and technique

### Decision-making and critical thinking

- Choose the best weight ball, position of the hoops and number of attempts to challenge yourself
- Set yourself realistic and achievable goals
- Keep re-evaluating and setting new goals

### Self-management

- Set up the challenge quickly and efficiently
- Challenge yourself to your maximum ability
- Focus on improving your own personal best
- Don't give up or cheat if the challenge gets difficult
- Maximise your activity time, allowing enough time to recover between attempts

# Shot put 6

## ■ Equipment

Shot of various weights, shot circle or cones, tape measure

## ■ Challenge

- Place 4 cones down as a throwing area (approx 2m x 2m) or use a shot put circle
- Stand in the throwing area/shot put circle facing side on to the direction of the throw
- Using a shot (choose your weight), perform a standing or side-shift put (choose your technique) for distance
- Ask someone to mark your distance with a cone
- Make further attempts to try to beat your best distance
- Measure and record your best distance and the weight of shot as a future target to improve upon

## ■ Technique tips *(for right-handed throwers)*

### Grip and hold
- Hold the shot at the base of your three middle fingers, supported by your thumb and little finger
- The shot must be held on the shoulder close to the chin
- The elbow of your putting arm should be kept high
- Think 'clean palm, dirty neck'

### Side-shift
- Stand at the back of the circle, facing sideways on to the direction of the put
- Bend your right leg and lower your upper body in preparation for the shift
- Push off your right leg and shift sideways into the middle of the circle
- At the end of the shift, pull your right leg under your body and place your left foot at the front of the circle
- Your upper body should remain low

### Release
- Position your feet with your right foot in the middle of the circle, your left foot at the front of the circle and your right heel in line with your left toe
- Your chin, knee and toe should be directly in line, one above the other, with your upper body low and your weight backwards
- Start the put by pushing your right hip towards the direction of the put

© 2011 Kevin Morgan, *Athletics Challenges*, Routledge.

- Push your chest forward and lift your body upwards
- Your right shoulder should follow and the arm should be 'last and fast'
- Extend your fingers to complete the put

## Health and safety

- Warm-up correctly before starting to throw (see warm-ups section)
- Do not complete this challenge unless a **teacher is supervising**
- Ensure everyone is in a safe position before you start to throw
- Communicate clearly with the person measuring before you start to throw

## Life skills

### Communication and interpersonal

- Communicate in a co-operative and friendly manner with others
- Encourage others to challenge themselves and achieve the best distance they can
- Give others positive and constructive feedback on their effort and technique

### Decision-making and critical thinking

- Choose the best weight shot to challenge yourself
- Set yourself realistic and achievable goals
- Keep re-evaluating and setting new goals

### Self-management

- Challenge yourself to your maximum ability
- Focus on improving your own personal best
- Don't give up or cheat if the challenge gets difficult

# Discus 1

### ■ Equipment

Discus/rubber discus, cones, tape measure

### ■ Challenge

- Work in groups of 4–5
- Place 2 cones down as a starting line about 10m apart and then a further 2 cones at the same width apart every 5m for up to 50m as shown below

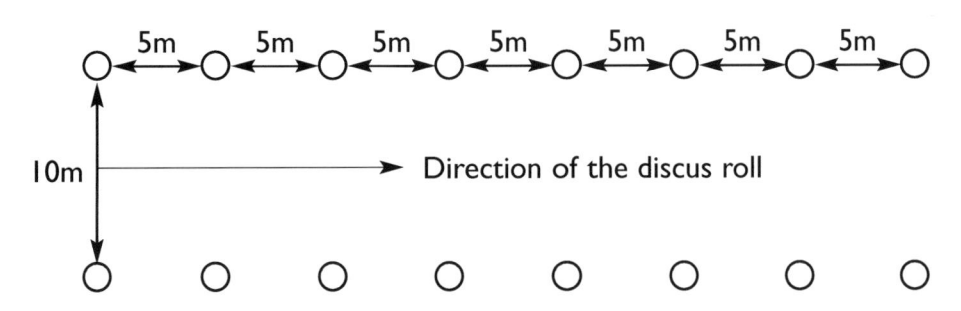

- From behind the starting line, roll the discus for distance
- Ask someone to mark the distance with a cone
- Make further attempts to try to beat your best distance
- Measure and record your best distance as a future target to improve upon

### ■ Technique tips

- Stand facing the direction of the roll
- Hold the discus by the pads of your fingertips, your thumb resting against the side
- Bend your knees and swing your arm back
- Keep your arm straight and to the side of your body
- Swing your arm forwards and release the discus to roll along the ground
- The discus should roll out of the front of your hand in a clockwise direction
- Your index finger should be the last finger in contact with the discus

© 2011 Kevin Morgan, *Athletics Challenges*, Routledge.

## Health and safety

- Warm-up correctly before starting to throw (see warm-ups section)
- Ensure that you communicate with the person marking your roll and that he/she is in a safe position before you start to roll the discus
- Ensure that you have plenty of space either side of you when rolling
- Carry the discus back safely to the throwing line between attempts

## Life skills

### Communication and interpersonal

- Communicate in a co-operative and friendly manner with others
- Encourage others to challenge themselves and achieve the best distance they can
- Give others positive and constructive feedback on their effort and technique

### Decision-making and critical thinking

- Set yourself realistic and achievable goals
- Keep re-evaluating and setting new goals

### Self-management

- Set up the challenge quickly and efficiently
- Challenge yourself to your maximum ability
- Focus on improving your own personal best
- Don't give up or cheat if the challenge gets difficult
- Maximise your activity time, allowing enough time to recover between attempts

# Discus 2

## ■ Equipment

Rubber discus/rubber quoit/bean bag/plastic hoop, 4 cones, tape measure

## ■ Challenge

- Place 2 cones down as a throwing line
- Sit behind the line facing the direction of the throw in straddle-sit position
- Using a rubber discus/quoit/bean bag/hoop, perform a sitting discus (straight-arm sling) throw for distance
- Ask someone to mark the distance with a cone
- Make further attempts to try to beat your personal best distance
- Measure and record your best distance as a future target to improve upon
- Repeat the process from a kneeling position facing the direction of the throw

## ■ Technique tips

- Hold the discus with your palm facing down, your arm straight and at shoulder height in front of your body
- Rotate your upper body backwards keeping a straight arm throughout
- Lead the throw with your chest, then shoulder, and the arm 'last and fast'
- Use your non-throwing arm to assist rotation
- Focus on the principles of 'low to high', 'slow to fast' and transfer of weight from 'back to front'

## Health and safety

- Warm-up correctly before starting to throw (see warm-ups section)
- Ensure that you communicate with the person marking your throw and that he/she is in a safe position before you start to throw
- Ensure that you have plenty of space either side of you when throwing
- Carry the discus back safely to the throwing line between attempts

## Life skills

### Communication and interpersonal

- Communicate in a co-operative and friendly manner with others
- Encourage others to challenge themselves and achieve the best distance they can
- Give others positive and constructive feedback on their effort and technique

### Decision-making and critical thinking

- Set yourself realistic and achievable goals
- Keep re-evaluating and setting new goals

### Self-management

- Set up the challenge quickly and efficiently
- Challenge yourself to your maximum ability
- Focus on improving your own personal best
- Don't give up or cheat if the challenge gets difficult
- Maximise your activity time, allowing enough time to recover between attempts

# Discus 3

### ■■■ Equipment

Rubber discus/rubber quoit/bean bag/plastic hoop, 3 cones, tape measure

### ■■■ Challenge

- Place 2 cones as a throwing line
- Stand behind the line facing side on to the direction of the throw
- Using a rubber discus/quoit/bean bag/hoop, perform a standing discus (straight-arm sling) throw for distance
- Ask someone to mark the distance with a cone
- Make further attempts to try to beat your personal best distance
- Measure and record your best distance as a future target to improve upon
- Repeat the process, starting facing away from the direction of the throw and then stepping back into the throwing stance

### ■■■ Technique tips

- Hold the discus with your palm facing down, your arm straight and at shoulder height in front of your body
- Bend your knees and rotate your upper body backwards, keeping a straight arm throughout
- Extend your legs and drive your hips towards the direction of the throw
- Your hips are followed by your chest and your arm should be 'last and fast'
- Focus on the principles of 'low to high', 'slow to fast', 'legs first arm last' and transfer of weight from 'back to front'

© 2011 Kevin Morgan, *Athletics Challenges*, Routledge.

## Health and safety

- Warm-up correctly before starting to throw (see warm-ups section)
- Ensure that you communicate with the person marking your throw and that he/she is in a safe position before you start to throw
- Ensure that you have plenty of space either side of you when throwing
- Carry the discus back safely to the throwing line between attempts

## Life skills

### Communication and interpersonal

- Communicate in a co-operative and friendly manner with others
- Encourage others to challenge themselves and achieve the best distance they can
- Give others positive and constructive feedback on their effort and technique

### Decision-making and critical thinking

- Set yourself realistic and achievable goals
- Keep re-evaluating and setting new goals

### Self-management

- Set up the challenge quickly and efficiently
- Challenge yourself to your maximum ability
- Focus on improving your own personal best
- Don't give up or cheat if the challenge gets difficult
- Maximise your activity time, allowing enough time to recover between attempts

# Discus 4

### ■ Equipment

Rubber discus/rubber quoit/bean bag, 2 cones, 4 plastic hoops

### ■ Challenge

- Work in groups of 4–5
- Place 2 cones as a throwing line and 4 hoops as targets (choose your distances and positions)
- Stand behind the line facing side on to the direction of the throw
- Using a rubber discus/rubber quoit/bean bag, perform a series of standing discus (straight-arm sling) throws for accuracy, using the hoops as targets
- Devise a scoring system and decide on the number of throws allowed
- Make further attempts to try to beat your best score
- Record the scoring system, number of throws and your individual or team score as a future target to improve upon

### ■ Technique tips

- Hold the discus with your palm facing down, your arm straight and at shoulder height in front of your body
- Bend your knees and rotate your upper body backwards, keeping a straight arm throughout
- Extend your legs and drive your hips towards the direction of the throw
- Your hips are followed by your chest and your arm should be 'last and fast'
- Focus on the principles of 'low to high', 'slow to fast', 'legs first arm last' and transfer of weight from 'back to front'

## Health and safety

- Warm-up correctly before starting to throw (see warm-ups section)
- Ensure that you communicate with the person marking your throw and that he/she is in a safe position before you start to throw
- Ensure that you have plenty of space either side of you when throwing
- Carry the discus back safely to the throwing line between attempts

## Life skills

### Communication and interpersonal

- Communicate in a co-operative and friendly manner with others
- Encourage others to challenge themselves and achieve the best distance they can
- Give others positive and constructive feedback on their effort and technique

### Decision-making and critical thinking

- Choose the best position of the hoops and number of attempts to challenge yourself
- Set yourself realistic and achievable goals
- Keep re-evaluating and setting new goals

### Self-management

- Set up the challenge quickly and efficiently
- Challenge yourself to your maximum ability
- Focus on improving your own personal best
- Don't give up if the challenge gets difficult
- Maximise your activity time, allowing enough time to recover between attempts

# Discus 5

### ■■■ Equipment

Rubber discus/rubber quoit/bean bag/plastic hoop, 5 cones, tape measure

### ■■■ Challenge

- Work in groups of 4–5
- Place 4 cones as a throwing area (approx 2m x 2m) or use a discus circle
- Stand at the back of the throwing area/discus circle facing away from the direction of the throw
- Using a rubber discus/quoit/bean bag/hoop, perform a full rotational discus turn and throw for distance
- Ask someone to mark the distance with a cone
- Make further attempts to try to beat your best distance
- Measure and record your best distance as a future target to improve upon

### ■■■ Technique tips *(for right-handed throwers)*

- Rotate your throwing arm as far to the right as possible
- Shift your body weight momentarily over your right foot, with your legs slightly bent
- Pivot your body weight around your left foot
- Rotate on the balls of your feet, towards the direction of the throw
- Leave the discus trail behind your body
- Pick up your right foot and place it in the middle of the circle/throwing area
- Pick up your left foot and place it in the throwing stance at the front of the circle
- When your feet are in the throwing stance, powerfully extend your legs
- Drive your hips towards the direction of the throw
- Your hips are followed by your chest and your arm should be 'last and fast'
- Reverse your feet to stop the forward momentum of your body
- Focus on the principles of 'low to high', 'slow to fast', 'legs first arm last' and transfer of weight from 'back to front'

© 2011 Kevin Morgan, *Athletics Challenges*, Routledge.

## Health and safety

- Warm-up correctly before starting to throw (see warm-ups section)
- Ensure that you communicate with the person marking your throw and that he/she is in a safe position before you start to throw
- Ensure that you have plenty of space either side of you when throwing
- Carry the discus back safely to the throwing line between attempts

## Life skills

### Communication and interpersonal

- Communicate in a co-operative and friendly manner with others
- Encourage others to challenge themselves and achieve the best distance they can
- Give others positive and constructive feedback on their effort and technique

### Decision-making and critical thinking

- Set yourself realistic and achievable goals
- Keep re-evaluating and setting new goals

### Self-management

- Set up the challenge quickly and efficiently
- Challenge yourself to your maximum ability
- Focus on improving your own personal best
- Don't give up if the challenge gets difficult
- Maximise your activity time, allowing enough time to recover between attempts

# Discus 6

### ■■■ Equipment

Discus of various weights, discus circle or cones, tape measure

### ■■■ Challenge

- Place 4 cones down as a throwing area (approx 2m x 2m) or use a discus circle
- Stand at the front of the throwing area/discus circle facing side on to the direction of the throw
- Using a discus (choose your weight), perform a standing discus throw for distance
- Ask someone to mark the distance with a cone
- Make further attempts to try to beat your personal best distance
- Measure and record your best distance as a future target to improve upon
- Repeat the process, starting facing away from the direction of the throw and then stepping back into the throwing stance

### ■■■ Technique tips *(for right-handed throwers)*

**Grip**
- Hold the discus by the pads of your fingertips, your thumb resting against the side of the discus

**Wind up**
- Start facing sideways on to the direction of the throw, with your right foot placed in the middle of the circle and your left foot at the front of the circle
- Your right heel should be in line with your left toe
- Your legs should be slightly bent
- Rotate your shoulders and discus throwing arm as far to the right as possible
- Your chin, knee and toe should be directly in line, one above the other, with your upper body low and your weight backwards

**Throw and reverse**
- Powerfully extend your legs
- Drive your hips towards the direction of the throw
- Follow your hips with your chest and your arm should be 'last and fast'
- Release the discus out of the front of your hand, off the index finger, spinning in a clockwise direction

© 2011 Kevin Morgan, *Athletics Challenges*, Routledge.

## Health and safety

- Warm-up correctly before starting to throw (see warm-ups section)
- Do not complete this challenge unless a **teacher is supervising**
- **Do not** attempt a **full discus turn** and throw unless you have the **use of a throwing cage**
- Ensure everyone is in a safe position before you start to throw
- Communicate clearly with the person measuring before you start to throw

## Life skills

### Communication and interpersonal

- Communicate in a co-operative and friendly manner with others
- Encourage others to challenge themselves and achieve the best distance they can
- Give others positive and constructive feedback on their effort and technique

### Decision-making and critical thinking

- Choose the best weight discus to challenge yourself
- Set yourself realistic and achievable goals
- Keep re-evaluating and setting new goals

### Self-management

- Challenge yourself to your maximum ability
- Focus on improving your own personal best
- Don't give up or cheat if the challenge gets difficult

# Javelin 1

### ■ Equipment

Weighted ball or soccer/basketball, 4 cones, tape measure

### ■ Challenge

- Place 2 cones as a throwing line
- Sit behind the line facing the direction of the throw with your legs out straight in front of you or in straddle-sit position
- Using a weighted ball (choose your weight) or soccer/basketball, perform a two-handed sitting 'pull' throw (from behind your head) for distance
- Ask someone to mark the distance with a cone
- Make further attempts to try to beat your personal best distance
- Measure and record your best distance as a future target to improve upon
- Repeat the process from a kneeling position facing the direction of the put

### ■ Technique tips

- Hold the ball with two hands behind your head
- Throw the ball using a soccer-style 'pull' throw
- Arch your back to assist the throw
- Release the ball above your head at about a 45-degree angle
- Follow through with your arms
- Focus on the principles of 'low to high' and 'slow to fast'

## ■ Health and safety

- Warm-up correctly before starting to throw (see warm-ups section)
- Ensure that you communicate with the person marking your throw and that he/she is in a safe position before you start to throw
- Ensure that you have plenty of space either side of you when throwing
- Carry or roll the ball back safely to the throwing line between attempts

## ■ Life skills

### Communication and interpersonal

- Communicate in a co-operative and friendly manner with others
- Encourage others to challenge themselves and achieve the best distance they can
- Give others positive and constructive feedback on their effort and technique

### Decision-making and critical thinking

- Choose the best weight ball to challenge yourself
- Set yourself realistic and achievable goals
- Keep re-evaluating and setting new goals

### Self-management

- Set up the challenge quickly and efficiently
- Challenge yourself to your maximum ability
- Focus on improving your own personal best
- Don't give up or cheat if the challenge gets difficult
- Maximise your activity time, allowing enough time to recover between attempts

# Javelin 2

### ■ Equipment

Weighted ball or soccer/basketball, 4 cones, tape measure

### ■ Challenge

- Place 2 cones as a throwing line
- Stand behind the line facing the direction of the throw with your feet shoulder-width apart
- Using a weighted ball (choose your weight) or soccer/basketball, perform a two-handed standing 'pull' throw (from behind your head) for distance
- Ask someone to mark the distance with a cone
- Make further attempts to try to beat your personal best distance
- Measure and record your best distance as a future target to improve upon
- Repeat the process using a 'step in' to the throw

### ■ Technique tips

- Hold the ball with two hands behind your head
- Throw the ball using a soccer-style 'pull' throw
- Bend your knees and arch your back to assist the throw
- Release the ball above your head at about a 45-degree angle
- Follow through with your arms
- Check the forward momentum of your body
- Focus on the principles of 'low to high', 'slow to fast', 'legs first arm last' and transfer of weight from 'back to front'

## Health and safety

- Warm-up correctly before starting to throw (see warm-ups section)
- Ensure that you communicate with the person marking your throw and that he/she is in a safe position before you start to throw
- Ensure that you have plenty of space either side of you when throwing and that there is no chance of the ball hitting anyone else
- Carry or roll the ball back safely to the throwing line between attempts

## Life skills

### Communication and interpersonal

- Communicate in a co-operative and friendly manner with others
- Encourage others to challenge themselves and achieve the best distance they can
- Give others positive and constructive feedback on their effort and technique

### Decision-making and critical thinking

- Choose the best weight ball to challenge yourself
- Set yourself realistic and achievable goals
- Keep re-evaluating and setting new goals

### Self-management

- Set up the challenge quickly and efficiently
- Challenge yourself to your maximum ability
- Focus on improving your own personal best
- Don't give up or cheat if the challenge gets difficult
- Maximise your activity time, allowing enough time to recover between attempts

# Javelin 3

### ■ Equipment

Weighted ball or soccer/basketball, 2 cones, 4 plastic hoops

### ■ Challenge

- Work in groups of 4–5
- Place 2 cones as a throwing line and 4 hoops as targets (choose your distances and positions)
- Stand behind the line facing the direction of the throw
- Using a weighted ball (choose your weight) or soccer/basketball, perform a series of two-handed standing 'pull' throws (from behind your head) for accuracy, using the hoops as targets
- Devise a scoring system and decide on the number of throws allowed
- Make further attempts to try to beat your best score
- Record the scoring system, number of throws and your individual or team score as a future target to improve upon

### ■ Technique tips

- Hold the ball with two hands behind your head
- Throw the ball using a soccer-style 'pull' throw
- Bend your knees and arch your back to assist the throw
- Release the ball above your head at about a 45-degree angle
- Follow through with your arms
- Check the forward momentum of your body
- Focus on the principles of 'low to high', 'slow to fast', 'legs first arm last' and transfer of weight from 'back to front'

## Health and safety

- Warm-up correctly before starting to throw (see warm-ups section)
- Ensure that you communicate with the person marking your throw and that he/she is in a safe position before you start to throw
- Ensure that you have plenty of space either side of you when throwing
- Carry or roll the ball back safely to the throwing line between attempts

## Life skills

### Communication and interpersonal

- Communicate in a co-operative and friendly manner with others
- Encourage others to challenge themselves and achieve the best score they can
- Give others positive and constructive feedback on their effort and technique

### Decision-making and critical thinking

- Choose the best weight ball, position of the hoops and number of attempts to challenge yourself
- Set yourself realistic and achievable goals
- Keep re-evaluating and setting new goals

### Self-management

- Set up the challenge quickly and efficiently
- Challenge yourself to your maximum ability
- Focus on improving your own personal best
- Don't give up or cheat if the challenge gets difficult
- Maximise your activity time, allowing enough time to recover between attempts

# Javelin 4

## ▪ Equipment

Weighted ball or soccer/basketball, 4 cones, tape measure

## ▪ Challenge

- Place 2 cones as a throwing line
- Stand behind the line facing away from the direction of the throw, one foot forward and one back and the ball to the side of your rear knee
- Using a weighted ball (choose your weight) or soccer/basketball, perform a two-handed 'lift-turn and throw' for distance
- Ask someone to mark the distance with a cone
- Make further attempts to try to beat your personal best distance
- Measure and record your best distance as a future target to improve upon

## ▪ Technique tips *(for right-handed throwers)*

- Hold the ball in two hands to the right side of your right knee
- Place your left foot behind you in a wide throwing stance
- To start the throw, turn quickly on the balls of your feet to face the direction of the throw whilst keeping your arms extended behind your body
- Try to make a 'bow' position with your body by pushing your hips forwards
- Pull your arms through very fast above your shoulders
- Drive your body up and over a straight left leg
- Release the ball above your head
- Focus on the principles of 'low to high', 'slow to fast', 'legs first arm last' and transfer of weight from 'back to front'

## Health and safety

- Warm-up correctly before starting to throw (see warm-ups section)
- Ensure that you communicate with the person marking your throw and that he/she is in a safe position before you start to throw
- Ensure that you have plenty of space either side of you when throwing
- Carry or roll the ball back safely to the throwing line between attempts

## Life skills

### Communication and interpersonal

- Communicate in a co-operative and friendly manner with others
- Encourage others to challenge themselves and achieve the best distance they can
- Give others positive and constructive feedback on their effort and technique

### Decision-making and critical thinking

- Choose the best weight ball to challenge yourself
- Set yourself realistic and achievable goals
- Keep re-evaluating and setting new goals

### Self-management

- Set up the challenge quickly and efficiently
- Challenge yourself to your maximum ability
- Focus on improving your own personal best
- Don't give up or cheat if the challenge gets difficult
- Maximise your activity time, allowing enough time to recover between attempts

# Javelin 5

## ■ Equipment

Foam javelin/bean bag/small ball/large foam ball, 4 cones, tape measure

## ■ Challenge

- Place 2 cones as a throwing line
- Stand behind the line facing the direction of the throw with one foot ahead of the other
- Holding the javelin/bean bag/ball in one hand above your shoulder, with your palm up and arm fully extended, perform a one-handed standing 'pull' throw for distance
- Ask someone to mark the distance with a cone
- Make further attempts to try to beat your personal best distance
- Measure and record your best distance as a future target to improve upon
- Repeat the process using a 2/3-step run-up into the throw

## ■ Technique tips *(for right-handed throwers)*

- Step out with your left leg into a wide throwing stance, with your heel contacting the ground first
- Your body should be tilted backwards and your arm fully extended
- Rotate your right knee and hip towards the direction of the throw
- Follow your hips with your chest, making a 'bow' position with your body
- Pull your throwing arm through very fast above your shoulder
- Drive your body up and over a straight left leg
- Release the ball above your head
- After release, bring your right leg forward and place it in front of your left leg
- Focus on the principles of 'low to high', 'slow to fast', 'legs first arm last' and transfer of weight from 'back to front'

© 2011 Kevin Morgan, *Athletics Challenges*, Routledge.

## ▬ Health and safety

- Warm-up correctly before starting to throw (see warm-ups section)
- Ensure that you communicate with the person marking your throw and that he/she is in a safe position before you start to throw
- Ensure that you have plenty of space either side of you when throwing
- Carry or roll the ball back safely to the throwing line between attempts

## ▬ Life skills

### Communication and interpersonal

- Communicate in a co-operative and friendly manner with others
- Encourage others to challenge themselves and achieve the best distance they can
- Give others positive and constructive feedback on their effort and technique

### Decision-making and critical thinking

- Set yourself realistic and achievable goals
- Keep re-evaluating and setting new goals

### Self-management

- Set up the challenge quickly and efficiently
- Challenge yourself to your maximum ability
- Focus on improving your own personal best
- Don't give up or cheat if the challenge gets difficult
- Maximise your activity time, allowing enough time to recover between attempts

# Javelin 6

### ■ Equipment

Javelins of various weights, javelin run-up area or cones, tape measure

### ■ Challenge

- Place cones as a run-up area or use a javelin run-up
- Stand in the run-up area holding the javelin (choose your weight)
- Perform a javelin throw for distance from a standing position or using a short run-up (3–5 strides)
- Ask someone to mark your distance with a cone
- Make further attempts to try to beat your best distance
- Measure and record your best distance and the weight of javelin as a future target to improve upon

### ■ Technique tips *(for right-handed throwers)*

**Grip**
- Hold the javelin in the centre of your palm with the index finger to the rear of the binding, or use a 'V' grip between your index and second fingers

**Approach**
- Stand facing the direction of the throw, with your hips and shoulders facing forwards,
- Hold the javelin back to full arm's length, the tip pointing slightly upwards towards the direction of the throw
- Start your approach

**Cross-step**
- On your second-to-last stride, place your right leg in front of your left leg to tilt your upper body backwards, keeping your arm as far back as possible
- Step out with your left leg into a wide throwing stance, with your heel contacting the ground first

**Throw**
- Rotate your right knee and hip towards the direction of the throw
- Follow your hips with your chest, making a bow position of your body
- Pull your throwing arm through fast above your shoulder
- Release the javelin in front of your head

- After release, bring your right leg forward and place it in front of your left, to stop you going over the line
- Your right shoulder should follow and the arm should be 'last and fast'

## Health and safety

- Warm-up correctly before starting to throw (see warm-ups section)
- Do not complete this challenge unless a **teacher is supervising**
- Ensure everyone is in a safe position before you start to throw
- Communicate clearly with the person measuring before you start to throw

## Life skills

### Communication and interpersonal

- Communicate in a co-operative and friendly manner with others
- Encourage others to challenge themselves and achieve the best score they can
- Give others positive and constructive feedback on their effort and technique

### Decision-making and critical thinking

- Choose the best weight javelin to challenge yourself
- Decide whether to do a standing throw or 3–5-stride run-up
- Set yourself realistic and achievable goals
- Keep re-evaluating and setting new goals

### Self-management

- Challenge yourself to your maximum ability
- Focus on improving your own personal best
- Don't give up or cheat if the challenge gets difficult

# Hammer 1

### ■ Equipment

Weighted ball or soccer/basketball, 3 cones, tape measure

### ■ Challenge

- Place 2 cones as a throwing line
- Stand behind the line facing the direction of the throw holding a weighted ball (choose your weight) or soccer/basketball in two hands between your legs
- Perform a standing two-handed underarm throw for distance
- Ask someone to mark the distance with a cone
- Make further attempts to try to beat your personal best distance
- Measure and record your best distance as a future target to improve upon

### ■ Technique tips

- Stand with your legs apart holding the ball in two hands between your legs
- Swing the ball forwards and upwards
- Bend your knees to start and extend them powerfully to assist the throw
- Keep your back flat and your head up
- Keep your arms straight throughout the throw
- Focus on the principles of 'low to high', 'slow to fast' and 'legs first arms last'

## ■ Health and safety

- Warm-up correctly before starting to throw (see warm-ups section)
- Ensure that you communicate with the person marking your throw and that he/she is in a safe position before you start to throw
- Ensure that you have plenty of space either side of you when throwing
- Carry or roll the ball back safely to the throwing line between attempts

## ■ Life skills

### Communication and interpersonal

- Communicate in a co-operative and friendly manner with others
- Encourage others to challenge themselves and achieve the best distance they can
- Give others positive and constructive feedback on their effort and technique

### Decision-making and critical thinking

- Choose the best weight ball to challenge yourself
- Set yourself realistic and achievable goals
- Keep re-evaluating and setting new goals

### Self-management

- Set up the challenge quickly and efficiently
- Challenge yourself to your maximum ability
- Focus on improving your own personal best
- Don't give up or cheat if the challenge gets difficult
- Maximise your activity time, allowing enough time to recover between attempts

# Hammer 2

### ■■■ Equipment

Weighted ball or soccer/basketball, 3 cones, tape measure

### ■■■ Challenge

- Place 2 cones as a throwing line
- Stand behind the line facing away from the direction of the throw holding a weighted ball (choose your weight) or soccer/basketball in two hands between your legs
- Throw the ball backwards over your head for distance
- Ask someone to mark the distance with a cone
- Make further attempts to try to beat your personal best distance
- Measure and record your best distance as a future target to improve upon

### ■■■ Technique tips

- Stand with your legs apart holding the ball in two hands between your legs
- Swing the ball backwards over your head
- Bend your knees to start and extend them powerfully to assist the throw
- Keep your back flat and your head up
- Keep your arms straight throughout the throw
- Release the ball above your head
- Focus on the principles of 'low to high', 'slow to fast' and 'legs first arms last'

© 2011 Kevin Morgan, *Athletics Challenges*, Routledge.

## Health and safety

- Warm-up correctly before starting to throw (see warm-ups section)
- Ensure that you communicate with the person marking your throw and that he/she is in a safe position before you start to throw
- Ensure that you have plenty of space either side of you when throwing
- Carry or roll the ball back safely to the throwing line between attempts

## Life skills

### Communication and interpersonal

- Communicate in a co-operative and friendly manner with others
- Encourage others to challenge themselves and achieve the best distance they can
- Give others positive and constructive feedback on their effort and technique

### Decision-making and critical thinking

- Choose the best weight ball to challenge yourself
- Set yourself realistic and achievable goals
- Keep re-evaluating and setting new goals

### Self-management

- Set up the challenge quickly and efficiently
- Challenge yourself to your maximum ability
- Focus on improving your own personal best
- Don't give up or cheat if the challenge gets difficult
- Maximise your activity time, allowing enough time to recover between attempts

# Hammer 3

### ■ Equipment

Weighted ball or soccer/basketball, 3 cones, tape measure

### ■ Challenge

- Place 2 cones as a throwing line
- Sit behind the line facing away from the direction of the throw in straddle-sit position holding a weighted ball (choose your weight) or soccer/basketball in two hands to the side of your body
- Perform a sitting two-handed 'heave' throw over one shoulder for distance
- Ask someone to mark the distance with a cone
- Make further attempts to try to beat your personal best distance
- Measure and record your best distance as a future target to improve upon

### ■ Technique tips *(for right-handed throwers)*

- 'Heave' the ball from outside your right knee over your left shoulder
- Keep your arms straight throughout the throw
- Let go of the ball above your left shoulder
- Throw from low to high
- Turn your upper body to follow the throw
- Focus on the principles of 'low to high' and 'slow to fast'

## Health and safety

- Warm-up correctly before starting to throw (see warm-ups section)
- Ensure that you communicate with the person marking your throw and that he/she is in a safe position before you start to throw
- Ensure that you have plenty of space either side of you when throwing
- Carry or roll the ball back safely to the throwing line between attempts

## Life skills

### Communication and interpersonal

- Communicate in a co-operative and friendly manner with others
- Encourage others to challenge themselves and achieve the best distance they can
- Give others positive and constructive feedback on their effort and technique

### Decision-making and critical thinking

- Choose the best weight ball to challenge yourself
- Set yourself realistic and achievable goals
- Keep re-evaluating and setting new goals

### Self-management

- Set up the challenge quickly and efficiently
- Challenge yourself to your maximum ability
- Focus on improving your own personal best
- Don't give up or cheat if the challenge gets difficult
- Maximise your activity time, allowing enough time to recover between attempts

# Hammer 4

### ▪▪▪ *Equipment*

Weighted ball or soccer/basketball, 3 cones, tape measure

### ▪▪▪ *Challenge*

- Place 2 cones as a throwing line
- Kneel behind the line facing away from the direction of the throw holding a weighted ball (choose your weight) or soccer/basketball in two hands to the side of your body
- Perform a kneeling two-handed 'heave' throw over one shoulder for distance
- Ask someone to mark the distance with a cone
- Make further attempts to try to beat your personal best distance
- Measure and record your best distance as a future target to improve upon

### ▪▪▪ *Technique tips* (for right-handed throwers)

- 'Heave' the ball from outside your right knee over your left shoulder
- Keep your arms straight throughout the throw
- Let go of the ball above your left shoulder
- Throw from low to high
- Turn your upper body to follow the throw
- Focus on the principles of 'low to high', 'slow to fast' and 'hips first arms last'

© 2011 Kevin Morgan, *Athletics Challenges*, Routledge.

## Health and safety

- Warm-up correctly before starting to throw (see warm-ups section)
- Ensure that you communicate with the person marking your throw and that he/she is in a safe position before you start to throw
- Ensure that you have plenty of space either side of you when throwing
- Carry or roll the ball back safely to the throwing line between attempts

## Life skills

### Communication and interpersonal

- Communicate in a co-operative and friendly manner with others
- Encourage others to challenge themselves and achieve the best distance they can
- Give others positive and constructive feedback on their effort and technique

### Decision-making and critical thinking

- Choose the best weight ball to challenge yourself
- Set yourself realistic and achievable goals
- Keep re-evaluating and setting new goals

### Self-management

- Set up the challenge quickly and efficiently
- Challenge yourself to your maximum ability
- Focus on improving your own personal best
- Don't give up or cheat if the challenge gets difficult
- Maximise your activity time, allowing enough time to recover between attempts

# Hammer 5

### ▪▪▪ Equipment

Weighted ball or soccer/basketball, 3 cones, tape measure

### ▪▪▪ Challenge

- Place 2 cones as a throwing line
- Stand behind the line facing away from the direction of the throw holding a weighted ball (choose your weight) or soccer/basketball in two hands to the side of your body
- Perform a standing two-handed 'heave' throw over one shoulder for distance
- Ask someone to mark the distance with a cone
- Make further attempts to try to beat your personal best distance
- Measure and record your best distance as a future target to improve upon

### ▪▪▪ Technique tips *(for right-handed throwers)*

- 'Heave' the ball from outside your right knee over your left shoulder
- Bend your knees to start and extend them powerfully to assist the throw
- Keep your back flat and your head up
- Keep your arms straight throughout the throw
- Let go of the ball above your left shoulder
- Throw from low to high
- Turn your upper body to follow the throw
- Focus on the principles of 'low to high', 'slow to fast', 'legs first arms last' and transfer of weight from 'back to front'

## ▰ Health and safety

- Warm-up correctly before starting to throw (see warm-ups section)
- Ensure that you communicate with the person marking your throw and that he/she is in a safe position before you start to throw
- Ensure that you have plenty of space either side of you when throwing
- Carry or roll the ball back safely to the throwing line between attempts

## ▰ Life skills

### Communication and interpersonal

- Communicate in a co-operative and friendly manner with others
- Encourage others to challenge themselves and achieve the best distance they can
- Give others positive and constructive feedback on their effort and technique

### Decision-making and critical thinking

- Choose the best weight ball to challenge yourself
- Set yourself realistic and achievable goals
- Keep re-evaluating and setting new goals

### Self-management

- Set up the challenge quickly and efficiently
- Challenge yourself to your maximum ability
- Focus on improving your own personal best
- Don't give up or cheat if the challenge gets difficult
- Maximise your activity time, allowing enough time to recover between attempts

# Hammer 6

### ■■■ Equipment

Soft indoor hammers/rubber quoits tied on a rope, 2 cones, 4 plastic hoops

### ■■■ Challenge

- Work in groups of 4–5
- Place 2 cones as a throwing line and 4 plastic hoops as targets (choose your distances and positions)
- Stand behind the line facing away from the direction of the throw
- Using a soft indoor hammer/rubber quoits on a rope, perform a series of hammer-style 'heave' throws for accuracy, using the hoops as targets
- Devise a scoring system and decide on the number of throws allowed
- Make further attempts to try to beat your best score
- Record the scoring system, number of throws and your individual or team score as a future target to improve upon

### ■■■ Technique tips *(for right-handed throwers)*

- Stand facing away from the direction of the throw
- Hold the handle of the rope in two hands to the side of your right leg, with your left hand under your right hand
- Swing the hammer around your head and release it over your left shoulder
- Keep your arms straight at the end of the throw
- Throw from low to high
- Turn your upper body to follow the throw
- Focus on the principles of 'low to high', 'slow to fast', 'legs first arms last' and transfer of weight from 'back to front'

© 2011 Kevin Morgan, *Athletics Challenges*, Routledge.

## ■ Health and safety

- Warm-up correctly before starting to throw (see warm-ups section)
- Ensure everyone is in a safe position before you start to throw
- Ensure that you have plenty of space either side of you when throwing
- Carry the hammer back safely to the throwing line between attempts

## ■ Life skills

### Communication and interpersonal

- Communicate in a co-operative and friendly manner with others
- Encourage others to challenge themselves and achieve the best score they can
- Give others positive and constructive feedback on their effort and technique

### Decision-making and critical thinking

- Choose the best position of the hoops and number of attempts to challenge yourself
- Set yourself realistic and achievable goals
- Keep re-evaluating and setting new goals

### Self-management

- Set up the challenge quickly and efficiently
- Challenge yourself to your maximum ability
- Focus on improving your own personal best
- Don't give up or cheat if the challenge gets difficult
- Maximise your activity time, allowing enough time to recover between attempts

# Section 3: Peer teaching sheets

## Teacher notes

The purpose of this section is to promote peer teaching, where students work in pairs with one as the performer and the other as the observer who offers feedback. The feedback is based on the written criteria and illustrations on the resource sheets and is given immediately, thus increasing the chances of improving and performing correctly. This teaching method aims to improve technical understanding and social and communication skills through learning how to give and receive feedback from peers. The teacher's role during the performances is to observe the performers and the observers, but to communicate with the observer only, so that they do not interfere with their role.

The teacher selects the subject matter and the criteria sheets for the observations and organises the logistics of the lesson. The introductory explanation should focus on the need for immediate feedback to improve performance and the fact that the teacher is unable to achieve this in a full-class situation. The other key factor in the introduction should be based on how to give positive and constructive feedback to each other and the role of the performer and the observer. The performer's role is to complete the task and initiate questions with the observer. The observer needs to refer to the criteria sheet, observe the performance, compare the performer against the criteria, draw conclusions about the accuracy of the performance and offer feedback. Success in this respect is evidenced when students are able to communicate with each other whilst exhibiting patience, tolerance and emotional sensitivity in addition to technical understanding.

Before the students start to work in pairs, the teacher should demonstrate or explain the technical model and provide a clear explanation of how to use the criteria sheet as a source of feedback. Students can be paired in various ways, but as social interaction is a primary aim, it is important to change pairings between lessons so that students also get to work with others in the class. During performances, the teacher's role is to move from one observer to another, offering feedback, assisting them with the criteria on the sheets and answering any questions, whilst interacting with the observers only. The key focus for the teacher at this stage is to observe and listen for technical accuracy, to improve communication and interpersonal skills and to ensure that students rotate roles between performer and observer. At the end of the episode the teacher should recap on the technical aspects on the criteria sheet and offer feedback to the whole class on the role of the observers.

The following set of criteria sheets include a technical breakdown for a variety of track and field athletics tasks. These criteria sheets should be photocopied and given out to

## ATHLETICS CHALLENGES ■ ■ ■ ■

students for them to refer to and complete whilst observing their partner's performance. It is recommended that the students have had previous experience of the practical techniques on the task criteria sheets on which to base their observations. Following the completion of the peer teaching episode, the completed sheets should be handed to the performer and kept in order to build up a technical profile of their athletic performances and to give them areas to work on to improve their techniques.

# ■ ■ ■ SPRINT STARTS ■ ■ ■

Performer's name.................................................................... Date..........................................................

Observer's name..............................................................................................................................

1. In your pair, decide who will first be the performer and observer
2. The performer repeatedly practises the task and receives feedback from the observer
3. The observer provides feedback to the performer using the illustrations and technique criteria listed below
4. When giving feedback, first acknowledge what was done correctly, and then offer corrective feedback about the errors
5. Tick 'yes' or 'no' to identify whether the criteria were correctly performed and, if not, identify areas for future improvement
6. Switch roles following a set number of repetitions or duration, as instructed by the teacher

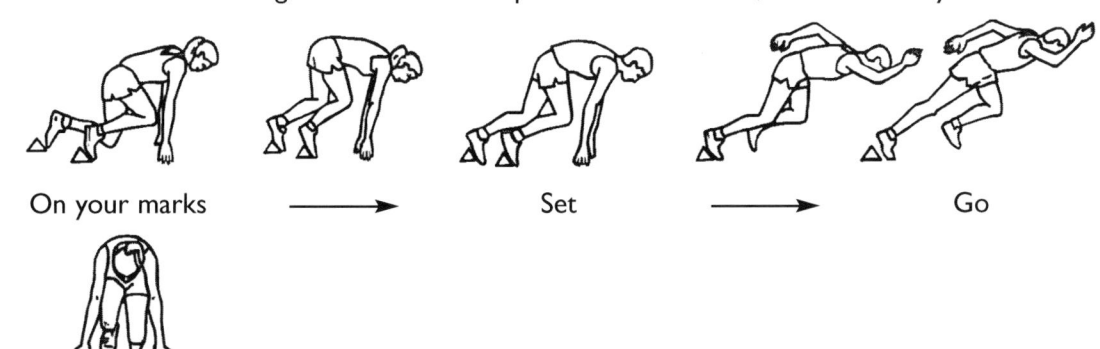

On your marks → Set → Go

| TECHNIQUE CRITERIA | YES | NO | AREAS FOR IMPROVEMENT |
|---|---|---|---|
| **ON YOUR MARKS** | | | |
| Front foot 1.5 to 2 feet behind the line | | | |
| Rear knee placed level with the front foot | | | |
| Body weight resting equally on rear knee and hands | | | |
| Hands placed behind the line, forming a 'V' with your fingers and thumb | | | |
| Arms shoulder-width apart | | | |
| Shoulders slightly ahead of the hands | | | |
| Look at the ground about 1m ahead of the line | | | |
| **SET** | | | |
| Hips raised slightly higher than the shoulders | | | |
| Shoulders ahead of the hands | | | |
| **GO** | | | |
| Strong push off the front leg | | | |
| Knee of the rear leg pulled forwards quickly | | | |
| Powerful pumping action with the arms | | | |
| Body angle remaining low for acceleration | | | |

© 2011 Kevin Morgan, *Athletics Challenges*, Routledge.

# ■■■ SPRINTING ■■■

**Performer's name**............................................................ **Date**...........................................................

**Observer's name**............................................................................................................................

1. In your pair, decide who will first be the performer and observer
2. The performer repeatedly practises the task and receives feedback from the observer
3. The observer provides feedback to the performer using the illustrations and technique criteria listed below
4. When giving feedback, first acknowledge what was done correctly, and then offer corrective feedback about the errors
5. Tick 'yes' or 'no' to identify whether the criteria were correctly performed and, if not, identify areas for future improvement
6. Switch roles following a set number of repetitions or duration, as instructed by the teacher

| TECHNIQUE CRITERIA | YES | NO | AREAS FOR IMPROVEMENT |
|---|---|---|---|
| Upper body inclined slightly forward | | | |
| Head still, looking straight ahead | | | |
| Relaxed (no tension) neck, arms and shoulders | | | |
| No twisting of the shoulders and torso | | | |
| Arms bent at 90 degrees at the elbow and pumping powerfully forwards and backwards | | | |
| Each leg pushing powerfully off the ground | | | |
| High knee lift | | | |
| Running tall on the balls of the feet | | | |

© 2011 Kevin Morgan, *Athletics Challenges*, Routledge.

# SUSTAINED RUNNING

Performer's name................................................................ Date........................................................................

Observer's name................................................................................................................................................

1. In your pair, decide who will first be the performer and observer
2. The performer repeatedly practises the task and receives feedback from the observer
3. The observer provides feedback to the performer using the illustrations and technique criteria listed below
4. When giving feedback, first acknowledge what was done correctly, and then offer corrective feedback about the errors
5. Tick 'yes' or 'no' to identify whether the criteria were correctly performed and, if not, identify areas for future improvement
6. Switch roles following a set number of repetitions or duration, as instructed by the teacher

| TECHNIQUE CRITERIA | YES | NO | AREAS FOR IMPROVEMENT |
|---|---|---|---|
| Upright posture | | | |
| Head still, looking straight ahead | | | |
| Relaxed (no tension) neck, arms and shoulders | | | |
| Arm action balancing that of the legs | | | |
| Economical, easy stride length | | | |
| Push of the ground to extend the leg fully on each stride | | | |
| Fairly low knee lift to conserve energy | | | |

© 2011 Kevin Morgan, *Athletics Challenges*, Routledge.

Section 3

Peer teaching sheets

# ■■■ HURDLING ■■■

**Performer's name**................................................................ **Date**........................................

**Observer's name**...........................................................................................................

1. In your pair, decide who will first be the performer and observer
2. The performer repeatedly practises the task and receives feedback from the observer
3. The observer provides feedback to the performer using the illustrations and technique criteria listed below
4. When giving feedback, first acknowledge what was done correctly, and then offer corrective feedback about the errors
5. Tick 'yes' or 'no' to identify whether the criteria were correctly performed and, if not, identify areas for future improvement
6. Switch roles following a set number of repetitions or duration, as instructed by the teacher

| TECHNIQUE CRITERIA | YES | NO | AREAS FOR IMPROVEMENT |
|---|---|---|---|
| Fast sprint towards the hurdle | | | |
| Upper body leaning towards the hurdle at take-off | | | |
| Lead leg picked up, bent at the knee | | | |
| Heel of the lead leg pushed over the centre of the hurdle | | | |
| Body balanced by reaching forward with the opposite arm to the lead leg | | | |
| Trail leg swung to the side of the body, bent at the knee | | | |
| A full stride taken off the hurdle | | | |
| A minimum rise and fall of the body throughout | | | |

158 © 2011 Kevin Morgan, *Athletics Challenges*, Routledge.

# RELAYS
## Upsweep exchange

Performer's name......................................................... Date..................................................

Observer's name...........................................................

1. In your 3s or 4s, decide on who will first be the performer and observer
2. The performer repeatedly practises the task and receives feedback from the observer
3. The observer provides feedback to the performer using the illustrations and technique criteria listed below
4. When giving feedback, first acknowledge what was done correctly, and then offer corrective feedback about the errors
5. Tick 'yes' or 'no' to identify whether the criteria were correctly performed and, if not, identify areas for future improvement
6. Switch roles following a set number of repetitions or duration, as instructed by the teacher

| TECHNIQUE CRITERIA | YES | NO | AREAS FOR IMPROVEMENT |
|---|---|---|---|
| **Outgoing runner** | | | |
| Palm of the receiving hand presented facing towards the incoming runner | | | |
| 'V' between fingers and thumb to receive the baton | | | |
| Receiving arm held straight and still, at hip height | | | |
| A tight grip on the baton before sprinting away | | | |
| **Incoming runner** | | | |
| Baton passed with an upward-pushing motion into the outgoing runner's hand | | | |
| Nearest part of the baton placed firmly and as far as possible into the hand of the outgoing runner | | | |

© 2011 Kevin Morgan, *Athletics Challenges*, Routledge.

Section 3

# RELAYS
## Downsweep exchange

Peer teaching sheets

**Performer's name**.................................................. **Date**..................................

**Observer's name**........................................................................................................

1. In your 3s or 4s, decide on who will first be the performer and observer
2. The performer repeatedly practises the task and receives feedback from the observer
3. The observer provides feedback to the performer using the illustrations and technique criteria listed below
4. When giving feedback, first acknowledge what was done correctly, and then offer corrective feedback about the errors
5. Tick 'yes' or 'no' to identify whether the criteria were correctly performed and, if not, identify areas for future improvement
6. Switch roles following a set number of repetitions or duration, as instructed by the teacher

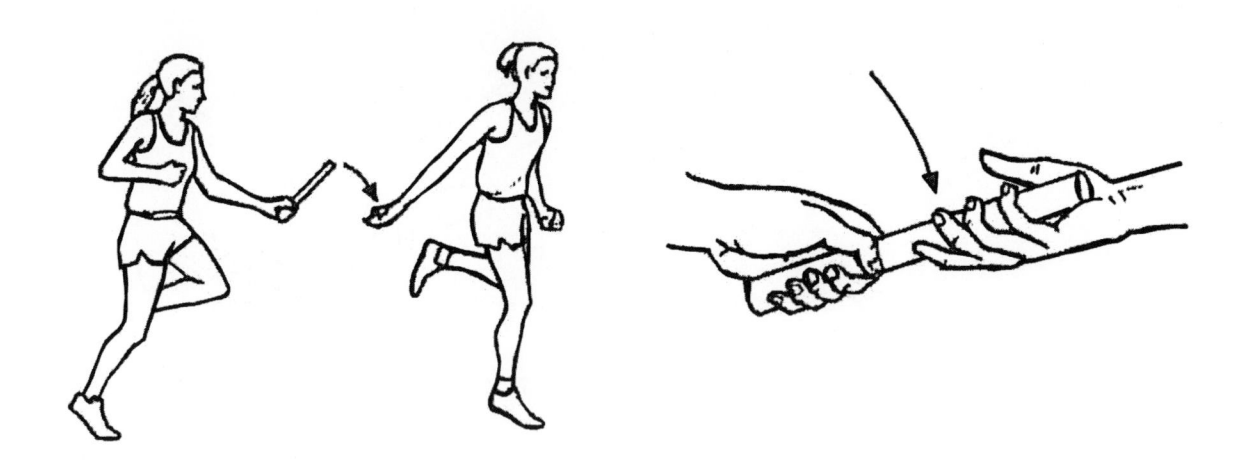

| TECHNIQUE CRITERIA | YES | NO | AREAS FOR IMPROVEMENT |
|---|---|---|---|
| **Outgoing runner** | | | |
| Palm of the receiving hand presented facing upwards and backwards towards the incoming runner | | | |
| 'V' between fingers and thumb to receive the baton | | | |
| Receiving arm held straight and still, above hip height | | | |
| Tight grip on the baton before sprinting away | | | |
| **Incoming runner** | | | |
| Baton passed with a downward, forward-pushing motion into the outgoing runner's hand | | | |
| Furthest part of the baton placed firmly into the hand of the outgoing runner | | | |

© 2011 Kevin Morgan, *Athletics Challenges*, Routledge.

# LONG JUMP
## Stride jump

**Performer's name** ............................................................. **Date** ..................................................................

**Observer's name** ......................................................................................................................................

1. In your pair, decide on who will first be the performer and observer
2. The performer repeatedly practises the task and receives feedback from the observer
3. The observer provides feedback to the performer using the illustrations and technique criteria listed below
4. When giving feedback, first acknowledge what was done correctly, and then offer corrective feedback about the errors
5. Tick 'yes' or 'no' to identify whether the criteria were correctly performed and, if not, identify areas for future improvement
6. Switch roles following a set number of repetitions or duration, as instructed by the teacher

| TECHNIQUE CRITERIA | YES | NO | AREAS FOR IMPROVEMENT |
|---|---|---|---|
| Use of a checkmark for accuracy at the beginning of the run-up | | | |
| Good speed and sprinting form on the run up – relaxed, high knee lift and powerful leg drive | | | |
| Upright body position at take-off | | | |
| Take-off foot placed ahead of the hips | | | |
| Good height at take-off | | | |
| Non take-off leg and both arms driven upwards at take-off | | | |
| Extension of the leading leg to assume a stride position in the air | | | |
| Both legs extended forwards for landing | | | |
| Good landing without falling backwards | | | |

© 2011 Kevin Morgan, *Athletics Challenges*, Routledge.

# TRIPLE JUMP

Performer's name.................................................... Date.....................................................

Observer's name.........................................................................................................

1. In your pair, decide on who will first be the performer and observer
2. The performer repeatedly practises the task and receives feedback from the observer
3. The observer provides feedback to the performer using the illustrations and technique criteria listed below
4. When giving feedback, first acknowledge what was done correctly, and then offer corrective feedback about the errors
5. Tick 'yes' or 'no' to identify whether the criteria were correctly performed and, if not, identify areas for future improvement
6. Switch roles following a set number of repetitions or duration, as instructed by the teacher

Hop ⟶ Step ⟶ Jump

| TECHNIQUE CRITERIA | YES | NO | AREAS FOR IMPROVEMENT |
|---|---|---|---|
| Controlled speed and sprinting form on the run-up – relaxed, high knee lift and powerful leg drive | | | |
| **HOP PHASE** | | | |
| Strong forward drive off the take-off leg | | | |
| Upright body position and a flat horizontal trajectory (take-off angle) | | | |
| Leading (non-jumping) leg driven to horizontal and then swung back to the rear | | | |
| Thigh of the jumping leg lifted upwards to achieve a wide stride position in the air | | | |
| Jumping leg pushed forwards for landing and flexed ready for the next phase | | | |
| **STEP PHASE** | | | |
| A strong push off the back leg | | | |
| The thigh of the free leg driven forwards and upwards into a wide stride position | | | |
| Upright body position | | | |
| **JUMP PHASE** | | | |
| Leading (non-jumping) leg swung forwards | | | |
| Both legs extended forwards for landing | | | |

© 2011 Kevin Morgan, *Athletics Challenges*, Routledge.

# HIGH JUMP
## Fosbury flop

**Performer's name** .................................................. **Date** ..................................

**Observer's name** ..................................................

1. In your pair, decide on who will first be the performer and observer
2. The performer repeatedly practises the task and receives feedback from the observer
3. The observer provides feedback to the performer using the illustrations and technique criteria listed below
4. When giving feedback, first acknowledge what was done correctly, and then offer corrective feedback about the errors
5. Tick 'yes' or 'no' to identify whether the criteria were correctly performed and, if not, identify areas for future improvement
6. Switch roles following a set number of repetitions or duration, as instructed by the teacher

| TECHNIQUE CRITERIA | YES | NO | AREAS FOR IMPROVEMENT |
|---|---|---|---|
| Fast curved approach, the body leaning inwards away from the bar | | | |
| Take-off foot placed ahead of the body, slightly flexed at the knee | | | |
| Take-off an arm's distance away from the bar and a quarter of the crossbar's length in from the nearest upright | | | |
| Upwards drive directly off the jumping foot | | | |
| Leg nearest the bar swung upwards and then back towards the run-up with the knee bent | | | |
| Use of the arms to assist take-off | | | |
| Body turned to jump backwards over the bar | | | |
| Hips pushed upwards to clear the bar | | | |
| Once the seat has crossed the bar, legs extended to clear the bar and head and shoulders lifted | | | |
| Landing on the back and shoulders | | | |

© 2011 Kevin Morgan, *Athletics Challenges*, Routledge.

# SHOT PUT
## Standing put

**Section 3 – Peer teaching sheets**

**Performer's name** .................................................... **Date** ....................

**Observer's name** ................................................................................

1. In your pair, decide on who will first be the performer and observer
2. The performer repeatedly practises the task and receives feedback from the observer
3. The observer provides feedback to the performer using the illustrations and technique criteria listed below
4. When giving feedback, first acknowledge what was done correctly, and then offer corrective feedback about the errors
5. Tick 'yes' or 'no' to identify whether the criteria were correctly performed and, if not, identify areas for future improvement
6. Switch roles following a set number of repetitions or duration, as instructed by the teacher

| TECHNIQUE CRITERIA (for right handed throwers) | YES | NO | AREAS FOR IMPROVEMENT |
|---|---|---|---|
| Shot held at the base of the three middle fingers, supported by the thumb and little finger | | | |
| Shot held on the shoulder close to the chin | | | |
| Standing sideways on to the direction of the put | | | |
| The right foot placed in the middle of the circle and the left foot at the front of the circle | | | |
| The right hip driven towards the direction of the put, followed by the chest and right shoulder | | | |
| The arm pushed 'last and fast' | | | |
| Fingers extended to complete the put | | | |

© 2011 Kevin Morgan, *Athletics Challenges*, Routledge.

# DISCUS
## Standing throw

Section 3

Peer teaching sheets

Performer's name................................................................ Date...................................................................

Observer's name.................................................................................................................................

1. In your pair, decide on who will first be the performer and observer
2. The performer repeatedly practises the task and receives feedback from the observer
3. The observer provides feedback to the performer using the illustrations and technique criteria listed below
4. When giving feedback, first acknowledge what was done correctly, and then offer corrective feedback about the errors
5. Tick 'yes' or 'no' to identify whether the criteria were correctly performed and, if not, identify areas for future improvement
6. Switch roles following a set number of repetitions or duration, as instructed by the teacher

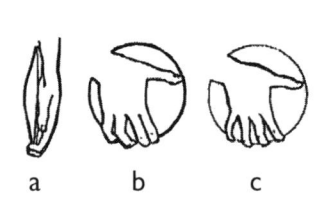

| TECHNIQUE CRITERIA (for right handed throwers) | YES | NO | AREAS FOR IMPROVEMENT |
|---|---|---|---|
| Discus held by the pads of the fingertips, thumb resting against the side (a) | | | |
| Index finger and second finger placed close together (b) or apart (c) | | | |
| Standing sideways on to the direction of the throw with the right foot placed in the middle of the circle and the left foot at the front of the circle | | | |
| Right heel in line with the left toe and legs slightly bent | | | |
| Shoulders and discus throwing arm rotated as far to the right as possible in the wind-up phase | | | |
| Chin, knee and toe in line, the upper body low and the body weight towards the back foot at the end of the wind-up phase | | | |
| Powerful extension of the legs to start the throw | | | |
| Hips driven towards the direction of the throw, followed by the chest | | | |
| The arm 'last and fast'. Discus released out of the front of the hand, off the index finger | | | |

© 2011 Kevin Morgan, *Athletics Challenges*, Routledge.

165

Section 3

Peer teaching sheets

# JAVELIN
## Standing throw

**Performer's name**.................................................. **Date**..................

**Observer's name**...................................................................................

1. In your pair, decide on who will first be the performer and observer
2. The performer repeatedly practises the task and receives feedback from the observer
3. The observer provides feedback to the performer using the illustrations and technique criteria listed below
4. When giving feedback, first acknowledge what was done correctly, and then offer corrective feedback about the errors
5. Tick 'yes' or 'no' to identify whether the criteria were correctly performed and, if not, identify areas for future improvement
6. Switch roles following a set number of repetitions or duration, as instructed by the teacher

| TECHNIQUE CRITERIA (for right handed throwers) | YES | NO | AREAS FOR IMPROVEMENT |
|---|---|---|---|
| Index finger grips the javelin to the rear of the binding (a) or | | | |
| Javelin gripped by the 'V' between index and second finger, to the rear of the binding (b) | | | |
| The javelin extended to full arm's length with the tip slightly raised | | | |
| Left leg stepping out into a wide throwing stance, heel contacting the ground first | | | |
| Body tilted backwards, arm fully extended | | | |
| Right knee and hip rotated vigorously towards the direction of the throw | | | |
| Hips followed by the chest, resulting in a 'bow' position of the body | | | |
| Javelin arm pulled through fast above the shoulder and the javelin released in front of the head | | | |

© 2011 Kevin Morgan, *Athletics Challenges*, Routledge.

# Section 4: Technical guidance sheets

## Teacher notes

The purpose of the technical guidance sheets is to allow students to work out and develop a good understanding of the correct principles and techniques of running, jumping and throwing. In order to guide students, a series of progressive practices and follow-up questions has been designed for a variety of track and field events. These sheets should be photocopied and given to the students to complete individually or in small groups during the lessons. The aim is that, through this process, the students will discover or consolidate key principles and/or techniques in order to improve their performances.

The teacher decides on the lesson objectives and activities and organises the logistics of the lessons. The students should participate in the activities individually, or in small groups, where they can be timed or measured in the different activities. By comparing their own personal best times or distances between progressive activities the correct principle or technical point should become clear to the students. Health and safety are the responsibility of the teacher and it is therefore important that students are closely monitored in the activities, particularly in the throwing events. Technical teaching progressions for activities such as sprint hurdling, relays and high jump should have preceded these activities in order to ensure the health and safety of the students. Safe equipment, such as a full high jump bed for the Fosbury flop, is also of paramount importance.

The role of the student learners is to complete the tasks and answer the questions. On occasions, due to the limited technical mastery or physical development of the students, progressive activities that should (according to the correct principles and techniques) improve the times or distances of the run, jump or throw may not do so. An example of this is the crouch sprint start time compared to the standing start time. If executed technically correctly, the crouch start should be faster due to the principle of staying low and driving forwards in the acceleration phase. However, if executed incorrectly, or if the student does not have sufficient leg power to drive effectively from a crouch start position, the standing start may be faster. In this instance, it is the teacher's responsibility to make the students aware of this through a questioning process that develops their understanding and learning of the principle or techniques involved. This process can, therefore, help the students to identify technical errors in their performances, which, if corrected, would improve their times or distances achieved.

## ATHLETICS CHALLENGES

The following points are the answers to the questions relating to the correct techniques and principles on the technical guidance sheets:

### Sprint starts
- Start with one foot ahead of the other
- Adopt a low body position to maximise acceleration from a static start
- Drive powerfully with your arms to maximise acceleration
- Start low and maintain a low body position with a slight forward lean

### Sprinting
- Pump your arms powerfully forwards and backwards
- Sprint with an upright posture and high hips
- Leg speed and stride length combine to maximise sprinting speed

### Sprint hurdles
- Run over the hurdles staying as low to them as you can safely
- Lead leg picked up bent at the knee and the heel pushed over the centre of the hurdle
- Bend your trailing leg at the knee and swing it to the side of your body over the hurdle
- Take the least number of strides in between the hurdles, whilst maintaining speed
- Establish a running rhythm and lead with the same leg each time

### Sprint relays
- Incoming runner should be at top speed when passing the baton
- Outgoing runner should be at top speed when receiving the baton
- Outgoing runner should use a checkmark to decide when to start and look forwards when receiving the baton to maximise speed

### Long jump
- Speed of run-up is directly related to the distance jumped
- Distance jumped is related to a combination of speed and height at take-off
- The body will rotate forwards in flight and the feet touch the ground earlier unless it is counteracted by bodily movements such as the 'hang' technique
- Once in flight, the flight path of the body cannot be changed but the position the feet touch the ground can be changed to maximise the distance jumped

### Triple jump
- Speed of run-up is directly related to the distance jumped, but there is an optimum speed that can be controlled and converted into jumping distance
- Distance jumped is related to a combination of speed and height at each take-off phase, with the hop being lowest and the jump phase highest
- Aim for equal distance phases to maximise overall distance
- Maintain speed between phases to maximise overall distance

### High jump
- Speed of run-up is directly related to the height jumped, but there is an optimum speed that can be controlled and converted into height
- A fast curved run-up in the Fosbury flop helps to rotate the jumper's body to go backwards over the bar
- Jump directly upwards off the take-off foot
- Use the arms to assist height at take-off

■ ■ ■ ■ **TECHNICAL GUIDANCE SHEETS**

**Shot put**
- Legs first arm last
- Transfer weight from back to front
- Start slow and finish fast
- Throw from low to high – optimum angle of release approximately 45 degrees
- Transfer momentum from the 'side shift' into the throw
- Correct sequence of the throw – legs, hip, chest, shoulder and arm

**Discus**
- Legs first arm last
- Transfer weight from back to front
- Start slow and finish fast
- Correct sequence of the throw – legs, hip, chest, shoulder and arm

**Javelin**
- Legs first arm last and transfer weight from back to front
- Correct sequence of the throw – legs, hip, chest, shoulder and arm
- Transfer momentum from the approach into the throw

# SPRINT STARTS

Name ..................................................................................................................................

- With someone to start and time you, perform the following sprint-start activities over 15/20m and record your time for each one
- Allow sufficient recovery time between sprints

| Activity | Time |
| --- | --- |
| 1. Standing upright, feet side-by-side and shoulder-width apart, hands by your sides | |
| 2. Standing upright, one foot ahead of the other, hands by your sides | |
| 3. Leaning forwards, one foot ahead of the other, hands by your sides | |
| 4. Leaning forwards, one foot ahead of the other, arms ready in the sprinting position | |
| 5. A crouch start, maintaining a low body position and slight forward lean during the sprint | |

## Questions

1. How did your time change from activities 1 to 2?
2. What key technical aspect of sprint starting does this identify?
3. How did your time change from activities 2 to 3?
4. What key technical aspect of sprint starting does this identify?
5. How did your time change from activities 3 to 4?
6. What key technical aspect of sprint starting does this identify?
7. How did your time change from activities 4 to 5?
8. What key technical aspect of sprint starting does this identify?
9. If you didn't improve your time from activities 4 to 5, think of possible reasons why not

# ■ ■ ■ SPRINTING ■ ■ ■

Name ........................................................................................................................................................

- With someone to start and time you, perform the following sprint activities over 20/30m, following a 'rolling start', and record your time for each one
- Allow sufficient recovery between sprints

| Activity | Time |
| --- | --- |
| 1. Sprinting with your arms by your sides | |
| 2. Sprinting whilst pumping your arms powerfully forwards and backwards | |
| 3. Sprinting whilst leaning forwards | |
| 4. Sprinting with an upright posture and high hips | |
| 5. Taking as many short, fast strides as possible | |
| 6. Increasing your stride length by lifting your knees and pushing off the ground, whilst maintaining a good leg speed | |

## Questions

1. How did your time change from activities 1 to 2?
2. What key technical aspect of sprinting does this identify?
3. How did your time change from activities 3 to 4?
4. What key technical aspect of sprinting does this identify?
5. How did your time change from activities 5 to 6?
6. What key principle of sprinting does this identify?

© 2011 Kevin Morgan, Athletics Challenges, Routledge.

# SPRINT HURDLING

Name ..................................................................................................................

- With someone to start and time you, perform the following sprint hurdle activities over 2/3 flights of hurdles and a distance of 20/30m and record your time for each one
- Allow sufficient recovery time between sprints

| | Activity | Time |
|---|---|---|
| 1. | Jumping over the hurdles, with an upright posture, allowing plenty of height to avoid hitting them | |
| 2. | Running over the hurdles, upper body leaning forwards, getting as low as possible without hitting them | |
| 3. | Taking numerous short, fast strides between the hurdles | |
| 4. | Taking the least number of long, fast strides between the hurdles as possible | |
| 5. | Running with no stride pattern/rhythm, leading with whichever leg happens to be the nearest to the hurdle at take-off | |
| 6. | Running with an established stride pattern/rhythm that allows you to lead with the same leg over each hurdle | |

## Questions

1. How did your time change from activities 1 to 2?
2. What key technical aspect of hurdling does this identify?
3. In order to achieve this, what is the best way to clear the hurdle with your lead and trailing legs?
4. How did your time change from activities 3 to 4?
5. What key principle of hurdling does this identify?
6. How did your time change from activities 5 to 6?
7. What key principle of hurdling does this identify?

© 2011 Kevin Morgan, Athletics Challenges, Routledge.

# SPRINT RELAYS

Name ................................................................................................................................

- With someone to start and time you, perform the following relay baton exchange activities over a distance of 30m (10m acceleration and 20m exchange zone – see below) and record your time for each one
- Allow sufficient recovery time between sprints

```
A |  10m acceleration  → B |    20m exchange box    → |
Start                                                  Finish
```

| Activity | Time |
|---|---|
| 1. The incoming runner (A) sprints the 10m acceleration phase. The outgoing runner (B) estimates when to start jogging away to receive the baton, whilst looking over his/her shoulder at the incoming runner | |
| 2. The incoming runner sprints the 10m acceleration phase. The outgoing runner uses a checkmark to start sprinting away to receive the baton, whilst looking over his/her shoulder at the incoming runner | |
| 3. The incoming runner sprints the 10m acceleration phase. The outgoing runner uses a checkmark to start sprinting away to receive the baton, whilst looking forwards and waiting for a 'hand' call | |

## Questions

1. How did your time change from activities 1 to 2?
2. What key principles of relay baton exchange does this identify?
3. If your time didn't improve from activities 1 to 2, adjust your checkmark and try again
4. How did your time change from activities 2 to 3?
5. What key principle of relay baton exchange does this identify?
6. If you didn't progressively improve your time from activities 1 to 3, think of possible reasons why not

© 2011 Kevin Morgan, *Athletics Challenges*, Routledge.

# LONG JUMP

Name ..........................................................................................................................................

- With someone to mark and measure your jumps, perform the following long jumps and record your distance for each one
- Allow sufficient recovery time between jumps

| Activity | Distance |
| --- | --- |
| 1. Standing long jump – take-off 1 foot, land on 2 | |
| 2. 3–5-stride run-up – take-off 1 foot, land on 2 | |
| 3. 9–11-stride run-up – take a big running stride off the board and land on 2 feet | |
| 4. 9–11-stride run-up – take a big running stride off the board, focus on height at take-off and land on 2 feet | |
| 5. 9–11-stride run-up – take a big 'high' running stride off the board, focus on pushing the hips forwards in flight and land on 2 feet | |
| 6. 9–11-stride run-up – take a big 'high' running stride off the board, focus on pushing the hips forwards in flight and the feet ahead of the hips for landing | |

## Questions

1. How did your distances change from activities 1 to 2 and 2 to 3?
2. What key principle of long-jumping does this identify?
3. How did your distance change from activities 3 to 4?
4. What key principle of long-jumping does this identify?
5. How did your distance change from activities 4 to 5?
6. What key principle of long-jumping does this identify?
7. How did your distance change from activities 5 to 6?
8. What key principle of long-jumping does this identify?
9. If you didn't progressively improve your distance from activities 3 to 6, think of possible reasons why not

© 2011 Kevin Morgan, Athletics Challenges, Routledge.

# TRIPLE JUMP

Name ...........................................................................................................................................

- With someone to mark and measure your jumps, perform the following triple jumps and record your distance for each one
- Allow sufficient recovery time between jumps

| Activity | Distance |
| --- | --- |
| 1. Standing triple jump – hop, stride, jump | |
| 2. 3–5-stride run-up – hop, stride, jump | |
| 3. 7–9-stride run-up – hop, stride, jump | |
| 4. 7–9-stride run-up – take a big low hopping stride off the board, a slightly higher stride and good height in the final jump phase | |
| 5. 7–9-stride run-up, focus on 3 equal distance phases (hop, stride, jump) | |
| 6. 7–9-stride run-up, focus on maintaining speed between the phases | |

## Questions

1. How did your distances change from activities 1 to 2 and 2 to 3?
2. What key principle of triple-jumping does this identify?
3. How did your distance change from activities 3 to 4?
4. What key principle of triple-jumping does this identify?
5. How did your distance change from activities 4 to 5?
6. What key principle of triple-jumping does this identify?
7. How did your distance change from activities 5 to 6?
8. What key principle of triple-jumping does this identify?
9. If you didn't progressively improve your distance from activities 2 to 6, think of possible reasons why not

© 2011 Kevin Morgan, Athletics Challenges, Routledge.

# ■■■ HIGH JUMP ■■■

Name .....................................................................................................................................

- With someone to mark and measure your jumps, perform the following Fosbury flop high jumps and record your height for each one
- Allow sufficient recovery time between jumps

| Activity | Distance |
|---|---|
| 1. Slow (jogging pace), straight 3-stride run-up | |
| 2. Fast straight, 3-stride run-up | |
| 3. Fast straight, 5-stride run-up | |
| 4. Fast curved, 5-stride run-up | |
| 5. Fast, J-shaped 7–9-stride run-up (straight for 2–4 strides and curved for the last 5 strides) | |
| 6. Fast, J-shaped 7–9-stride run-up (straight for 2–4 strides and curved for the last 5 strides), focus on jumping directly upwards and using the arms to assist height at take-off | |

## Questions

1. How did your height change from activities 1 to 2 and 2 to 3?
2. What key principle of high-jumping does this identify?
3. How did your height change from activities 3 to 4 and 4 to 5?
4. What key principle of Fosbury flop high-jumping does this identify?
5. How did your distance change from activities 5 to 6?
6. What key principles of high-jumping does this identify?
7. If you didn't progressively improve your distance from activities 2 to 6, think of possible reasons why not

# SHOT PUT

Name ........................................................................................................................................

- With someone to measure your throws, perform the following shot put activities and record your distance for each one
- Allow sufficient recovery time between throws

| | Activity | Distance |
|---|---|---|
| 1. | Standing put, facing front on to direction of the put, feet shoulder-width apart, no use of legs | |
| 2. | Standing put, facing front on to direction of put, feet shoulder-width apart, start with bent legs and extend them powerfully to put | |
| 3. | Standing put, facing sideways on to direction of put, weight on the back foot to start and an open stance – left toe and right heel in line (right-handed thrower) | |
| 4. | Standing put, facing sideways on to direction of put, weight on the back foot to start. Start slow and finish with the arm 'last and fast' | |
| 5. | Side-shift put, staying low in the shift and using the legs for power | |

## Questions

1. How did your distance change from activities 1 to 2?
2. What key principle of shot put does this identify?
3. How did your distance change from activities 2 to 3?
4. What key principle of shot put does this identify?
5. How did your distance change from activities 3 to 4?
6. What key principle of shot put does this identify?
7. How did your distance change from activities 4 to 5?
8. What key principle of shot put does this identify?
9. What is the correct sequence of body parts in the throw?
10. If you didn't progressively improve your distance from activities 1 to 5, think of possible reasons why not

© 2011 Kevin Morgan, *Athletics Challenges*, Routledge.

# DISCUS

Name ........................................................................................................................................

- With someone to measure your throws, perform the following discus activities and record your distance for each one
- Allow sufficient recovery time between throws

| Activity | Distance |
| --- | --- |
| 1. Standing throw, facing sideways on to the direction of the throw, no use of legs | |
| 2. Standing throw, facing sideways on to the direction of the throw, start with bent legs and extend them powerfully to throw | |
| 3. Standing throw, facing sideways on to the direction of the throw, weight on the back foot to start and an open stance – left toe and right heel in line (right-handed thrower) | |
| 4. Standing throw, facing sideways on to the direction of the throw, weight on the back foot to start. Start slow and finish with the arm 'last and fast' | |

## Questions

1. How did your distance change from activities 1 to 2?
2. What key principle of discus throwing does this identify?
3. How did your distance change from activities 2 to 3?
4. What key principle of discus throwing does this identify?
5. How did your distance change from activities 3 to 4?
6. What key principle of shot put does this identify?
7. What is the correct sequence of body parts in the throw?
8. If you didn't progressively improve your distance from activities 1 to 4, think of possible reasons why not

# JAVELIN

Name ..........................................................................................................................................

- With someone to measure your throws, perform the following javelin activities and record your distance for each one
- Allow sufficient recovery time between throws

| | Activity | Distance |
|---|---|---|
| 1. | Standing throw, one foot ahead of the other, throwing arm straight to start, hips facing the direction of the throw, upright posture, no use of legs | |
| 2. | Standing throw, throwing arm straight to start, hips facing the direction of the throw, upper body leaning backwards, weight on the back foot to start | |
| 3. | Standing throw, throwing arm straight to start, upper body leaning backwards, right leg slightly bent and turned out to the side (right-handed thrower), weight on the back foot, rotate right knee and hip forwards to throw | |
| 4. | Short approach (3/5 strides) with a cross-over step on the penultimate stride to get into the throwing position as in activity 3 above | |

## Questions

1. How did your distance change from activities 1 to 2?
2. What 2 key principles of javelin throwing does this identify?
3. How did your distance change from activities 2 to 3?
4. What key principle of javelin throwing does this identify?
5. How did your distance change from activities 3 to 4?
6. What key principle of javelin throwing does this identify?
7. If you didn't progressively improve your distance from activities 1 to 4, think of possible reasons why not

© 2011 Kevin Morgan, *Athletics Challenges*, Routledge.

# References

Ames, C. (1984) 'Competitive, co-operative and individualistic goal structures: A motivational analysis', in R. Ames and C. Ames (eds), *Research on motivation in education: Student motivation* (pp. 177–207). New York: Academic Press.

Ames, C. (1992) 'Achievement goals, motivational climate, and motivational processes', in G. Roberts (ed.), *Motivation in sport and exercise* (pp. 161–76). Champaign, IL: Human Kinetics.

Carpenter, P. J. and Morgan, K. (1999) 'Motivational climate, personal goal perspectives and cognitive and affective responses in Physical Education classes'. *European Journal of Physical Education*, 4, 31–44.

Epstein, J. L. (1989) 'Family structures and student motivation: A developmental perspective', in R. Ames and C. Ames (eds), *Research on motivation in education, Vol 3: Goals and Cognitions* (pp. 259–95), New York: Academic Press.

Fox, K. and Harris, J. (2003) 'Promoting physical activity through schools', in J. McKenna and C. Riddoch (eds), *Perspectives on health and exercise* (pp. 181–200). Basingstoke: Palgrave McMillan.

Gardner, H. (1993) *Multiple Intelligences*. New York: Basic Books.

Kay, W. (2003) Lesson planning with the NCPE 2000. The revised unit of work, *Bulletin of PE*, 39(1), 31–42.

Mandigo, J., Corlett, J., Sheppard, J. and Krohe, J. (2008) *Teaching life skills for understanding through games*. International TGfU conference, University of British Columbia, Vancouver, May 2008.

Morgan, K. (2000) 'Motivation in athletics lessons'. *British Journal of Teaching Physical Education*, 31(1), 16–18.

Morgan, K. (2003) 'Teaching Styles, Progression and Variety in Athletics Lessons'. *British Journal of Teaching Physical Education*, 34(1), 12–14.

Morgan, K. (2004) 'Developing Key Skills in KS2 Athletics'. *British Journal of Teaching Physical Education*, 35(2), 10–13.

Morgan, K. and Carpenter, P. J. (2002) 'Effects of manipulating the motivational climate in Physical Education lessons'. *European Physical Education Review*, 8(3), 207–29.

Morgan, K., Kingston, K. and Sproule, J. (2005) Effects of different teaching styles, on the teacher behaviours that influence motivational climate in physical education. *European Physical Education Review*, 11(3), 257–86.

Mosston, M. and Ashworth, S. (2002) *Teaching physical education*, 5th edn. San Francisco, CA: Benjamin Cummins.

Nicholls, J. G. (1978) 'The development of the concepts of effort and ability, perception of academic attainment, and the understanding that difficult tasks require more ability'. *Child Development*, 49, 3, 800–14.

Parish, E., Rudisill, M. E. and St. Onge, P. (2007) 'Mastery motivational climate: Influence on physical play and heart rate in African American toddlers'. *Research Quarterly for Exercise and Sport*, 78, 171–8.

Whitehead, M. (ed.) (2010) *Physical literacy throughout the lifecourse*. London: Routledge.